TO LEARN
WITH LOVE

A COMPANION
FOR SUZUKI
PARENTS

WILLIAM AND CONSTANCE STARR

Cover Design: William J. Starr, Jr.

Kingston Ellis Press

Library of Congress Cataloging in Publication Data: 83-081442
ISBN: 0-914425-00-5

First Printing March 1984
Second Printing October 1984
Third Printing April 1986

Published by Kingston Ellis Press
1014 Freemason Street
Knoxville, Tennessee 37917

To our dear children,
Kathleen, Teresa, Greg, Tim,
Judith, Bill, Michael, and David,
With gratitude
For the loving, living, and forgiving
That we have shared.

To the many children, parents, and teachers
Who've enriched our lives
With their love and friendship
Over these last twenty years.

And to Shinichi Suzuki
For the inspiration
That created an environment of learning with love.

"If love is deep, much can be accomplished".

William and Constance Starr

THE AUTHORS

William Starr made his debut as soloist with the Kansas City Philharmonic at the age of seventeen. He acquired two degrees and a Performer's Certificate at the Eastman School of Music and played first violin in the Rochester Philharmonic. While a member of the faculty at the University of Tennessee he was first violinist of the University String Quartet and concertmaster of the Knoxville Symphony, appearing as soloist fourteen times. In 1977-82 he served as Head of the Music Department. He is now an adjunct professor at the University of Colorado. His books, "Scored for Listening", a music appreciation text (Harcourt, Brace), "Music Scores Omnibus", a music anthology (Prentice Hall), and a music theory text, "Perceiving Music", (Harcourt, Brace), have been widely used in colleges since 1959. In 1972-74 Mr. Starr was a member of the Fulbright National Screening Committee for Strings, serving as its chairman in 1975. He began the Suzuki violin program at Tennessee in 1964, visiting Japan in 1967 and 1968-69. His Suzuki students performed at a conference of the World Organization for Human Potential in Philadelphia, the Music Educators' National Conference in Atlanta, the American Symphony Orchestra League national convention in Memphis, and toured Venezuela twice, appearing with the Venezuelan Symphony. His book, "The Suzuki Violinist" has been in demand by parents and teachers since its publication in 1976. A later book, "Twenty-Six Composers Teach the Violinist", is gaining wide use with advanced students. He has taught at all of the International Suzuki Conferences and in Canada, England, Australia, Venezuela, and Switzerland. One of the founders of the Suzuki Association of the Americas, he was its first president from 1972-74, and is chairman of the board of the recently formed International Suzuki Association.

Constance Starr studied piano at the Chicago Musical College and at Interlochen, where she was also principal violist of the orchestra. While earning a degree in piano performance at the Eastman School of Music, she was an active member of the Eastman Concert Bureau, appearing as soloist and assisting artist. She was both violist and pianist with the Knoxville Symphony, appearing five times as piano soloist. While playing viola in the University of Tennessee String Quartet, she also performed piano chamber music and served as part-time piano instructor in the music department. Because of their intense interest in early childhood education, the Starrs were co-founders of the Knoxville Montessori Association of which Ms. Starr served as first president. In 1971 she wrote, in collaboration with William Starr, a widely used text, "Practical Piano Skills", published by Wm. C. Brown and now in its third edition. Ms. Starr is writing a series of books called "The Music Road, A Journey in Music Reading". Volumes 1 and 2 have been enthusiastically received and Volume 3 is scheduled for 1984 release. In 1968-1969 Ms. Starr spent fourteen months in Japan with her husband and eight children, observing in depth the piano teaching of Haruko Kataoka and Shizuko Suzuki and making video tapes of student lessons and performances. She wrote an article in CLAVIER introducing Suzuki piano to the U.S. and gave the first workshops for piano teachers in the U.S. Students from her Suzuki piano program in Knoxville have won contests, appeared as soloists on two tours of Venezuela, on the Suzuki International Tour and at the International Conferences. She has served SAA as chairman of the piano committee and as piano editor of the Journal. A member of the piano faculty at four international conferences, she is actively sought after as clinician and teacher-trainer at institutes and workshops in the U.S. and abroad.

The Starrs have performed frequently on faculty recitals at Suzuki institutes and international conferences.

Preface

For a number of years we have been giving talks to parents at workshops and institutes throughout the country, sharing experiences and insights we have gained from our own family and from the families of students we have taught. At the same time we learned a great deal from the questions that were repeated by parents again and again and by their sharing possible solutions to problems that seem to exist universally! "How I wish there were more time to spend with you!" appreciative members of the audience frequently commented. "Why don't you write a book?" others suggested. And that was the spark that started our project!

We are neither child psychologists nor graduates in child development yet our large family and our introduction to Suzuki led us to read and study hundreds of books related to the child and his world.

Having taught and performed on our respective instruments for many years, having studied and adopted the Suzuki method as teachers and parents for a good number of those years, and having raised eight children—one of them still in the process—we have chalked up a lot of experience. That experience has included many errors, failures, successes and triumphs. It has contained pain and suffering, joy and enthusiasm in abundance. It has made us more knowledgeable human beings. But even more important, hopefully it has molded us into more loving, caring, and forgiving human beings.

Life is made up of many significant facets—like the characters in a play. Each role is an important part of the complex whole. Just as the Suzuki method deals with the whole child, not just his musical life, so "To Learn With Love" is not a book covering only musical pursuits. Each of the subjects covered is one we have considered important in a family's growth.

Suzuki has said "If love is deep much can be accomplished." In Willa Cather's "Death Comes to the Archbishop", the bishop affirms the same belief, "Where there is great love there are always miracles".

Suzuki has opened our minds and hearts to the fact that learning with love can be a great and glorious adventure—and that miracles can happen anywhere when that environment of love is surrounding us.

Notes About the Text

This book is a shared venture. Although we have collaborated on all of the material in this book, we have used italics to indicate the passages written by Connie, and roman type for Bill's writing. Regardless of who is designated as the writer, all of the text is the result of our cooperative efforts.

In regard to the perennial problem of 'he' and 'she', we have decided to mix their use. The student will be 'he' and the teacher 'she' for several chapters, then the pronouns will be reversed. This alteration continues throughout the book.

CONTENTS

The adult's idea that freedom consists in minimizing duties and obligations must be rejected. The foundation of education must be based on the following facts: That the joy of the child is in accomplishing things great for his age; that the real satisfaction of the child is to give maximum effort to the task at hand; that happiness consists in well directed activity of body and mind in the way of excellence; and that true freedom has, as its objective, service to society and to mankind consistent with the progress and happiness of the individual.

Maria Montessori

Learning: A Fascinating Process

The development of musical skills in children is a fascinating subject for study, but those of us teaching and parenting don't have access to much research in this area. Scientific studies of the growth of musical skills in children are almost non-existent. Measurement of success is obviously too complicated. If a child makes seven good serves out of ten in volley ball, we can all see and record the results; however, a student may play all the correct notes insofar as pitch and rhythm are concerned, only to be judged by a musician as deficient in dynamics, balance and phrasing. One can understand why studies are lacking in this area.

Fortunately, many of the principles of learning observed in other areas will help us in our work with children. Both the Suzuki parent and the Suzuki teacher can profit from a knowledge and understanding of the ways in which young children learn both motor and cognitive skills. Psychologists have done extensive research in these areas. Observations drawn from this research do have a bearing on problems we face in working with young children in music.

Although Suzuki says that he gave up reading books by psychologists some time ago, he did arrive at many of the same conclusions after his own extensive study of children. Such statements as "At age three children are unable to . . .", or "A four year old cannot comprehend. . . .", caused him to reject others' opinions and led him to study children directly himself.

Suzuki observed the learning habits of children. These observations and his reflections on them gave birth to his idea to apply the mother-tongue method to the teaching of music to small children. As his success tells us, he found that children have enormous potential for learning and that poor teaching, poor environment, and inadequate adult expectations have been the principal causes of limiting that potential.

Suzuki's Discovery, The Mother-Tongue Method

"All Japanese children speak Japanese!" exclaimed Suzuki to his friends one day. He had suddenly realized the astonishing fact that every normal child old enough to talk had been successfully educated by the mother-tongue method. "Children everywhere learn to speak their own tongues fluently which shows that they have a very high level of ability. The most successful example of the learning process is the mother-tongue method. Not only do normal children all over the world learn the basics of their mother-tongue without text, test, or classroom, but they also learn to speak the dialect with its often subtle nuances, and they are able to build an amazing vocabulary before they ever set foot in a school".

Natural Learning

The characteristics of the mother-tongue method are actually those of the child's natural learning period in every area, the period in which the child's intuitive learning ability is at its peak, and the period in which he is in the driver's seat controlling his advancement. It is only when the child learns to walk, to talk, and to use his hands for holding, grasping, and manipulating that he determines when he is ready to walk, talk, and use his hands. We should reflect on all of the aspects surrounding the development of these skills. What an exciting period of growth to observe!

It is obvious that the environment encourages such learning. Adult interest and praise are usually strong, the desire to imitate the adult and other children is powerful, and there are usually good models for observation. The child develops at his own rate, most often with a staggering number of repetitions.

Suzuki, in his approach, capitalizes on the principal features of the natural learning method. He stresses: 1) A favorable environment, with encouragement, interest, praise, and models of sight and sound to observe (listening to recordings is an important part of that

12

environment); 2) The awakening and growth of a desire to play a musical instrument; 3) Absence of stress, no problem with self-image; 4) A very slow rate of progress at the beginning; 5) Great number of repetitions; 6) Individual rates of progress; 7) Joy of learning; 8) Realization of potential of all.

Slow Rate of Progress. Many Repetitions

"Beginners learn so slowly. Same as mother-tongue. The baby does not say 'Mama' and then immediately speak many different words. No!", Suzuki says emphatically.

Lawther (1968) states that observations and experimental studies show a very slow rate of progress in primary or sensory-motor learning in young children. He calls attention to the youngster's need to automatize each activity before it can be integrated with another for a higher stage of learning. This process requires a great number of experiences.

Suzuki says, "The mother does not say to the child, 'You have said "Mama" enough times. Next word.' No. The child must repeat and repeat if he is to learn. Knowledge is not skill. Knowledge plus 10,000 times is skill."

Many studies of children report that they repeat, rework, and reiterate. When very young, they often repeat or try to repeat the same expression, phrase, or sentence over and over again. As many as seventy repetitions of a word, phrase, or sentence have been made in one period by a child. (Lawther, 1968)

Dr. Helen K. Billings, an innovative educator and the keynote speaker at the International Suzuki Conference in Amherst, Massachusetts in 1981, tells this anecdote in her book, "A Priceless Educational Advantage". "Once I observed a child trying to climb up one step! Thirty-seven times she tried and failed; but the thirty-eighth time she made it! And the look of joy and satisfaction on her face as she turned to survey the world from this hilltop position of one step was something that will always remain with me! I was well rewarded for waiting patiently, exerting great control and letting her do it herself. Such occurrences reveal the capacity of a child to become absorbed in a task and to persist."

LEARNING: A FASCINATING PROCESS

(A recording of Dr. Billings' book, "A Priceless Educational Advantage", read by Dr. Billings herself, is available on audio cassette tape. See Appendix.)

Researchers have found that even older children and adults need many repetitions to accomplish a skill.

Each time that I observed lessons in Haruko Kataoka's studio in Matsumoto, I became more excited by what I heard. On one particular day I sat quietly at the rear of the studio and watched students, parents, and observers come and go. Most of the time there were at least eight or ten people sitting behind the tables at the back of the room.

When we were in Japan five years before, I had been delighted by the playing of a four-year-old girl, Kaori Maruyama. Her performance of the first movement of Beethoven's Sonata, Opus 49, No. 2, was beautiful. Now I was hearing her again at age nine. During her lesson, as she was working on the Italian Concerto by Bach, an office secretary came in to notify Mrs. Kataoka of a phone call that must be answered immediately. Mrs. Kataoka left the room, and Kaori continued to work without interruption on a short, difficult passage that she had been asked to practice. She didn't turn away from the keyboard during Mrs. Kataoka's absence, but continued to practice without a pause. By the time Mrs. Kataoka returned, Kaori had repeated the passage thirty-five times!

Growth Rates. Maturation

It's odd that we parents who accept without question the fact that our children learn to talk and walk at different times forget all about this when our children begin any kind of formal training. Perhaps we accept each child's timetable for talking and walking because we know we can't do anything about it. How ridiculous we would feel trying to force a baby to say a new word!

When our first daughter, Kathleen, was born, we bought one of the first home tape recorders. It was an exciting toy. We were going to record all of our daughter's first words, or so we thought. We now have, in the family tape file, a ridiculously silly thirty-minute tape of Mommy, Daddy, and Grandma saying "Mama — Daddy — dog — me — boy — girl, etc." fifty or sixty times, followed by silence or the sound of Kathleen chewing on the microphone!

And her learning to walk! I must admit I was a little impatient when she took several steps holding tightly to one of my fingers, but steadfastly refused to walk by herself. I simply could not disengage my finger from that powerful grip! I tried to trick her. I gave her a stick to hold at one end while I held the other, then attempted to distract her so that I could let go. It never worked. As soon as I released the stick, she sat down immediately.

Later, I thought that I had succeeded in tricking Kathleen into walking. I handed her two baby food jars and told her, "Take these to Daddy." Imagine my surprise when she walked off, taking six confident steps! I know now that I had done nothing clever. She knew that the time was right. She was ready. The baby food jars and my request were merely coincidental!

Yes, during her natural learning period Kathleen was absolutely independent in determining her rate of progress, as were her many and varied younger siblings who all learned at different rates, but at rates that were uniquely their own. Teresa, our second daughter, for instance, was traveling fast and furiously at nine months, climbing everything in sight as well as walking. Tim, our second son, didn't start talking until he was over a year old, but when he started, it came in a torrent! It amazes us when we hear a parent proclaim, "They begin to walk at eleven months." We haven't the slightest idea when they should be expected to begin to walk. All of our children's rates of progress were so different that we became hopelessly confused. If someone asks one of us, "when do children . . . ?", we tell them to ask the parent of a single child!

Unfortunately, it seems that the child loses the unerring timetable guide that he possesses during the period in which he learns basic skills. Does he really know when he is ready to go on to the next step when he is studying math at school or violin at home? Do we teachers and parents really know when he is ready to move on? I call experienced teachers 'educated guessers' in this matter.

Kyoko Kawamoto, a gifted teacher who worked in Japan and in Knoxville for a few years, said, "Sometimes I take a big step with my students. If it works, I am happy. We save a lot of time. If it doesn't, I say, 'Let's go back and prepare you better for that step'. Then I try to determine how many small steps I may need to fill in."

Sensitivity to Each Child's Growth

You should discuss the rate of your child's growth with the teacher. In fact, this should be one of the most important topics of discussion between you. You should know why the teacher is doing what she is doing with your child. If you are concerned that Susie is being allowed to progress more rapidly than your Johnny and the reason for it is not obvious to you, you most certainly should talk to the teacher about this. If you ask that your child be allowed to move more quickly, your teacher may react defensively, perhaps with good reason. She may feel that the qualitative standards you have for your child are too low, and that you seem to be more concerned about keeping up with Susie rather than the good of your child. However, if your child is becoming uptight about his study and you report this, your teacher will most likely lessen the requirements as you request.

We teachers and parents need to keep reminding ourselves that ALL CHILDREN MATURE AT DIFFERENT RATES, and that assignments and expectations should reflect these differences. We must also remember the child's need for adequate repetition to automatize each activity as he progresses.

Growth Rates Change

Growth rates are by no means constant. "Once a slow learner, always a slow learner" is simply not true. We should not put a tag on the slow beginner. Remember the story Suzuki told in "Nurtured by Love" about the parakeet named Peeko Miyazawa? Peeko had to hear 3000 repetitions of the word 'Peeko' before he was able to say it, but only 200 repetitions of his family name, 'Miyazawa'. "Ability breeds ability", Suzuki says.

Suppose the owner had taken Peeko back to the shop after only 2700 repetitions of 'Peeko'. "This is a stupid parakeet. He'll never learn. I want another that learns at a reasonable rate". What would have happened to Peeko's development? What actually did happen was that Peeko, after learning to say his name, began to imitate everything he heard, even after only one hearing! I'm sure people marveled at Mr. Miyazawa's parakeet. Did he tell them that Peeko was an especially slow learner? Did anyone ever ask Winston Churchill when he learned to talk? . . . Or ask Jesse Owens when he learned to walk?

Initial Levels of Proficiency

Psychologists state that initial levels of proficiency are not valid for predicting future achievement levels in a specific endeavor. In Suzuki's speeches he often makes this point, mentioning a fine advanced student who is known to the audience, and recalling that student's slow beginnings. "I was a very slow beginner," said Yukari Tate, the brilliant fourteen-year-old soloist at the first appearance of the Japanese children at the Music Educators National Conference in Philadelphia in 1964.

Singer (1972) quoted research support for the observation that the relationship between initial and final status is quite low on more complex tasks. THIS IS ESPECIALLY TRUE WHERE ENOUGH TIME AND PRACTICE ARE ALLOWED FOR LEARNING TO OCCUR.

Many teachers have encountered parents who have asked, "Is there any test that you can give my child to determine whether or not he has innate musical ability?" Suzuki, confronted with such an inquiry, jokingly asks, "Did your child walk in here with you? Can he talk to you about studying the violin? If he can do both of these things, he has already demonstrated high ability."

In answer to the parental inquiry about a proficiency test, we can quote the observations of Singer (1972). "Ability tests of complex tasks involving both physical and personality variables are not of any practical value."

The Three Phases of Skill Learning

Psychologists mention three phases of skill acquisition (Robb, 1972):

1) In the first phase, the learner understands what he is supposed to do.

2) The second phase consists of meaningful practice with appropriate feedback.

3) The third and final phase is automatic execution. (When the movement pattern is largely automatic, the musician can concentrate on interpretation.)

First Phase of Learning

Suzuki's awareness of the first phase of learning is shown clearly in his approach. He is constantly telling his teachers that the mothers, and thus their children, should know exactly what the student is supposed to practice and how to practice it.

Mitsumasa Denda, an outstanding teacher in Nagano, says that mere demonstration and explanation are not enough. "I ask the student to play the passage that he is to work on at home several times at the lesson until I'm sure that he and the parent understand the objective and how to accomplish it."

It is up to you to find out from your teacher precisely what your child is expected to achieve. Never leave the studio without a clear picture of the goals for the week. Don't be afraid to say, "I don't understand . . . please explain again. . . . please show me."

Second Phase of Learning

The second phase of learning, consisting of meaningful practice with appropriate feedback, is often filled with shortcomings that seriously hamper learning. Because of its scope, meaningful practice will be discussed in the chapter entitled Practice.

Knowledge of results, or feedback, is considered by psychologists studying skill learning to be one of the most significant factors in practice. Authorities have long recognized (Oxendine, 1968) that the learner improved much more quickly if he received specific information about the relationship of his performance to his goal. Feedback is described in cybernetic theory (Wiener, 1950) as error information and is one of the most important variables controlling and regulating human behavior.

The archer sees his arrow strike the target to the left of the bullseye. The bowler sees his ball roll into the right gutter. The basketball player sees the ball bounce off the front edge of the hoop. The golfer watches his ball career off the fairway.

Knowledge of results, or feedback, in the above instances is automatic, instantaneous, and easily observed. Faults contributing to the errors mentioned above may not always be easily seen but the errors are perceived immediately.

In the study of a musical instrument, however, many errors can be made without the student being aware of them. To an extent, due to Suzuki's emphasis on listening to recordings, the Suzuki student does have a built-in error recognition system in that he notices when something he plays doesn't sound like the recording. A wrong note should leap out at him if he has listened enough. This, however, is not sufficient feedback. Parents need to provide additional information.

Appropriate Feedback from Parents

How should parents give their children appropriate feedback? To be most effective, the feedback must be meaningful to the child, specific in nature, and must be given immediately after he plays.

We should not, however, remain content with supplying him with feedback, but should endeavor to help him recognize his own feedback. We should assist him in observing his own sensory information from the task.

You might say, "Your bow is moving crookedly toward the fingerboard", and leave it at that. Better awareness training for him would be for you to draw the bow in a straight line, asking, "Can you feel the difference? Close your eyes and draw the bow. Without opening your eyes, tell me whether you think the bow was straight." After his response, you can ask him to open his eyes, and then tell him how the bow did move.

Most children do need help in learning to focus their own awareness on what they are doing as they play. It is possible, and so easy for them, to be a kind of 'middle man' between teacher and parent.

LEARNING: A FASCINATING PROCESS

Teacher tells parent what must be done, parent sees that child does it. The child can become a passive non-observer, totally uninvolved!

Asking questions of the students instead of telling them what is wrong or what needs change or improvement makes it necessary for the children to pay close attention or they cannot answer. For that reason I have done a great deal of questioning at lessons. If the tone is weak, I play a passage with a good singing tone, and then with a weak tone asking, "Which one did you like better?" After they have answered— and they do answer 'the first one' ninety-nine percent of the time—I ask, "Which one sounded like your tone?" If they have no idea I ask them to play again and then tell me what they think. We do this again and again if it is necessary until they are confident that they can trust their own feedback.

Parents can do similar things during practice at home. "After you play this passage, tell me whether it sounded like your recording." "Your teacher asked you to practice finger action. When you play this part tell me whether your fingers were lazy or active." "Does the rhythm in that part sound like your recording? Let's listen and then play it again. Tell me if it sounds the same." This kind of involvement cannot help but improve the climate of practice time and at the same time develop the student's trust in his ability to observe what he does.

I wish it were always easy to supply appropriate feedback. There are so many qualitative judgments to be made. You should work to become a keen observer and help your child to become one, too. Often children practice without any feedback except their own unskilled observations that everything is o.k., so they can get on with it. Of course, practice time is shorter and easier that way.

You should have confidence that you can improve as an observer not only in visual matters but also in aural perception. (Suzuki said that he puts tapes on the violin fingerboard so that the beginner's mother can see if the finger is in the right place and not have to rely on her ear to know whether the note is in tune!)

More on feedback can be found in the chapter on Concentration.

Third Phase of Learning

Automatic execution is found in the third phase of learning. Anyone seeing Suzuki's demonstrations with tour groups knows that his goal is automatic execution, not that performance should be automatic without musical sensitivity, but that the technical problems should be executed automatically. The large musical audience greeting Suzuki in Philadelphia at the Music Educators National Conference in 1964 was made well aware of this goal as he directed the youngsters to play a Vivaldi concerto. While they were playing, he asked them, "What is your name? How old are you? What city is this?" They answered without missing a note of the music.

In fact, Suzuki's whole program of reviewing pieces reinforces the principle of automatic execution. He has always been sensitive to the need for automatized activity, wherein the students gain great confidence in their abilities and are able to refine and develop their performances continually through constant review. Again, "Ability breeds ability."

Concert artists who are constantly performing in front of the public must have complete automatic execution. A good example of this is a story told about Artur Rubinstein, the famous concert pianist. After a performance with the Philadelphia Orchestra of the Concerto in B Flat by Brahms, an exuberant fan came backstage to see him. "Oh, Mr. Rubinstein, that was the most exquisite playing I have ever heard you do!"

Rubinstein smiled and replied gently, "Thank you. Before the performance I received a telephone call telling me of the birth of our son. Actually, I don't remember anything about the performance at all. . . . I wasn't aware of playing any of it!"

This is a case of a seasoned performer who had performed the work many times and whose whole body was programmed to artistic as well as technical excellence.

I remember Isaac Stern rehearsing the Prokofieff D Major Violin Concerto with Leonard Bernstein conducting. Stern was racing through a difficult passage in the last movement and talking to Bernstein at the same time without missing a beat! During intermission the air backstage was filled with difficult excerpts from violin concerti as the orchestral violinists congregated in twos and threes, trying to talk to each other while playing!

Parental Expectations

Wisely held and wisely expressed parental expectations can be extremely helpful to the child's growth. Nancy St. John, in a study done in 1972, found a significant correlation between mothers' and childrens' attitudes toward scholastic success. Maternal estimations and aspirations were found to be more optimistic than those of their children, but were also found to be better predictors of children's attitudes than family socio-economic status.

Unreasonable parental expectations, however, can be a stressful factor limiting a small child's development. Parental expectations must be transmitted in a loving, caring way that conveys to the child our belief in him and our respect for his feelings.

Margie, a bright four-year-old piano student, was elevated on a pedestal by her parents who spoke openly in front of her about her high IQ and her need for 'accelerated' instruction in the classroom . . . in this case, kindergarten! Margie believed that the love and approval she received was conditional, that it was based on her performance in all areas. Naturally she didn't want to jeopardize her position.

She had done very well, learning quickly, until we reached the point of putting hands together in Lightly Row. After two weeks of struggling with little sign of improvement she announced to me at her lesson that she didn't want to put hands together and she wasn't going to practice on it anymore. Realizing that meeting this head-on would probably have negative results, I quickly prayed for guidance! "O.K., Margie," I answered agreeably. "You can practice your left hand part and the melody separately. When you feel you're ready to practice them together, let me know."

About two weeks later she decided to risk it. Her desire to 'get on with it' was stronger than her fear of facing her apparent weakness. This same reluctance occurred whenever there was anything that couldn't be learned immediately after its introduction. Because I understood the terrific responsibility she had to live up to her parents' image of her, I tried to help her as much as I could by not pushing. Parental expecta-

tions that put a heavy burden on a child actually make her want to give up rather than strive for further goals.

When parental expectations are conveyed in the proper way the results can be far different. Alison began the study of violin at age four, the piano at age six. She was a lovely little girl, attentive and interested, with a beautiful spirit. Her mother spent a great deal of time with her, sacrificing time from her own activities without resentment. Indeed her mother showed nothing but pleasure and enthusiasm when she was involved with Alison's musical activities.

Nothing was too difficult for Alison. If somthing did not respond immediately to practice, her mother would say, "We're working on it. We'll get it soon." And Alison would!

Alison excelled academically as well as being a superior performer on both the violin and piano. Upon her graduation from high school, she gave a beautiful recital, playing both instruments. She is now a music major at the Indiana University School of Music, an excellent example of the child who is nurtured by a parent with wisely held and wisely expressed expectations.

In thinking about our children and in talking and working with them, we should always maintain a confident view of their potential. They may take a longer time than others of the same age to accomplish certain goals, but we owe it to them and to ourselves to keep an optimistic and enthusiastic attitude.

Teacher's Expectations

Suzuki says that he finds many examples of inadequate adult expectations limiting children's potential. "Even in Japan I must keep convincing mothers that their children have high abilities. When I started Talent Education I didn't know the extent of the potential of young children with the violin. I was convinced that they had great potential but I had no precise goal in mind. Gradually I began to expect that all children could play the Vivaldi A Minor Concerto very well. Then I raised my expectations to the Bach A Minor Concerto. And now I must raise my expectations again. It depends on how well we teach."

Many experienced teachers who've started working with the Suzuki approach have confessed that their expectations of their students' growth have increased a great deal and have been borne out by the students' consequent development.

Yamamura-sensei, an extremely successful teacher in Nagoya spoke of his change of attitude when he became a Suzuki teacher. "In my earlier days of teaching I was polite to a slow learner, but I know I must have conveyed my limited expectancy to the student. Now if a child doesn't learn well, instead of judging him to be untalented, I ask myself, 'How can I help this child unlock his abilities, abilities I know he must have?' "

In their book, "Pygmalion in the Classroom, Teacher Expectation and Pupils' Intellectual Development," Robert Rosenthal and Lenore Jacobson cite a study made by the Harvard-National Science Foundation. "In a certain elementary school 20% of the children were reported to their teachers as showing unusual potential for intellectual growth. The names of these children had been drawn out of a hat although tests had been administered to lead the teachers to believe the choice was being scientifically made. Eight months later these "magic" children showed significantly greater gains in IQ than the children who had not been singled out. The change in the teacher's expectation had led to an actual change in the intellectual peformance of these randomly selected children."

You may have heard the story about the teacher who was overjoyed when she received the roster of her new class. Next to the children's names were a series of numbers in the 130s and 140s. "They've given me the students with the high IQs!" she exulted. The class did exceedingly well as she expected. It wasn't until months later she found that the numbers were locker numbers!

Goals

Learners must have goals. The fact that the Suzuki repertoire is common to all students propels the youngsters onward as they desire to play the next piece they've heard on the recording and in performance by more advanced students. It is Suzuki's cherished hope that this will be the principal goal motivating students to practice and progress. This desire to play the next piece can get out of hand, however, if the parent allows the child to go ahead of the teacher's assignment. He may learn the piece with serious mistakes that will be very difficult to correct.

Constant dwelling on far-off goals does not provide the healthiest environment for learning a skill. The parent who has only distant goals such as "I hope my daughter will be concertmistress of the school orchestra when she grows up", "I want my son to win the youth talent contest", or "It would be wonderful if my daughter wins a scholarship to Juilliard!", may miss all the fun of watching her children develop day by day.

Mischa Elman, the celebrated Russian violinist, in an interview, urged students not to dwell too much on their aspirations to be concert artists. He compared learning to play the violin with the activity of a mountain climber. "The mountaineer doesn't spend much time and energy gazing at the far-off peak he is trying to ascend but rather devotes most of his attention to the problem of the next rock or crevass that is facing him." Elman assured students that when they did pause for self-appraisal, they would be delighted to see how far they had come, taking one hurdle at a time.

Habits

An adult or child generally approaches a skill-learning situation with a wide variety of habits already available. The swimmer, for instance, already knows how to kick, move his arms, and breathe in and out. These are all examples of what is called relatively well-developed 'serial' behavior.

The child approaching the study of violin, however, usually does not have a relevant repertory of habits. It is doubtful that he has had much experience holding something firmly between his chin and shoulder, looking to the left to watch something closely, holding his left hand up to the side and turned so that the little finger points to the face, grasping any object with the peculiarities of the bow hold, or moving the right arm so as to draw the bow in straight lines.

I feel that the bad habits developed by the beginning violin student are due principally to the fact that the child not only does not have relevant habits already available, as does the swimmer, but does have habits that seem related and so he uses them. He is accustomed to looking at objects closely by holding them down in front of him, so he wants to hold the violin that way. He is accustomed to holding fragile objects securely, or being told to, so he holds the violin neck firmly in his left fist and the bow firmly in his right fist. He generally moves his right arm in an arc, so he moves the bow crookedly. And so on. I think it helps to point this out, perhaps even to a small child. It certainly is helpful to parents to understand that many errors made by beginners are the result of natural inclinations. This is why Suzuki insists that beginners should move so slowly.

Since I play the viola as well as the piano, I can make a comparison. Extension of the pianist's arms and hands over the keyboard does not run counter to any previously acquired habits. He plays upon the keyboard and does not have to support the instrument as he plays. Only the fingers cannot rely upon past habits. It is doubtful that the child has had any experience using firm, independent fingers. He will need to develop this habit but he will not be hindered by a previous related habit.

Acquiring new habits may be difficult but is very valuable training for the child. Psychologists show that CHILDREN LEARN NEW HABITS WITH EASE OR DIFFICULTY DEPENDING UPON THE QUALITY AND QUANTITY OF THEIR PREVIOUS EXPERIENCE IN HABIT FORMATION.

Rate of Improvement

Both parent and child should know that the rate of improvement during practice on a specific complex task is by no means stationary. The rate of improvement is often very fast at the start. The first repetitions contribute a great deal to the mastery of the problem. Children are sometimes quite disturbed by the fact that the following repetitions seem to contribute increasingly less to the total performance.

This is one advantage of the Suzuki review work. In fact, Suzuki doesn't expect the student to have complete mastery of a piece before he goes on to the next one. Hundreds of follow-up repetitions are scattered through the student's practice days as he reviews earlier material.

These repetitions, contributing more slowly to the learning process, are not as stressful as they would be if the student were to do all of them immediately after the notes and fingering were learned. The refinement and growth are very gradual, perhaps not perceived by the child, yet very real, contributing significantly to the child's developing skill.

Plateaus

Another characteristic of the rate-of-learning curve that bothers all of us at times is that period of no observable improvement called a plateau. Plateaus are not always predictable, but teachers do witness their appearances at various points in the Suzuki study.

Researchers in motor learning say that plateaus appear when separate response components begin to emerge into continuous, smooth acts. At this time habits are being overlearned. The student is becoming freer and approaching automaticity, a state in which later learning becomes easier. Plateaus seem to be unavoidable, but if their nature is understood, the student will not become so discouraged and frustrated.

Suzuki's choice of literature provides some breathing points. Some pieces require no additional technical skills. The student feels he is learning more easily as he learns a new piece without realizing that it presents no new problems.

Positive and Negative Transfer

Transfer is an interesting aspect of the learning process. We most often think of it in a positive way, rejoicing when we notice that something learned earlier aids us in learning a similar skill. Children are especially delighted when they find that, because of something they have already learned, they are able to play quite easily similar passages in other works. "If you learn this part well," you may encourage your child," you'll not only be able to play it well but will also be able to play easily a part like it in another piece."

Understanding negative transfer is helpful to the student or parent who is wondering why the fingers persist in going down incorrectly. A good example of this is often encountered as the student starts Lightly Row after a long period on Twinkle. He plays open E, then down comes the third finger on the A string even though his ear tells him that this is not the right finger, that it should be the second finger following the open E. How helpful to the child if he knows why this happens! "Just look at the third finger! He's so well trained to come down after he hears the open E string. You'll have to tell him to wait this time, because in Lightly Row it's second finger's turn to play right after open E!"

A similar negative transfer takes place when the piano student has learned to play the left hand of Cuckoo and then proceeds to the left hand of Lightly Row. In Cuckoo the first two notes are fingered 5-3; in Lightly Row 5-1. Invariably when Lightly Row is first being practiced, the fingers come down 5-3. "You'll need to remind number three to wait this time," you can suggest. "His turn comes after the thumb in this piece."

In helping to erase well-established habits like this or even when first learning a fingering in a new piece, I find that asking the child to say the finger numbers aloud requires attentive thinking and results in fewer repetitions needed for accomplishment.

Reminiscence

Most teachers say they have had the following experience. A student plays. "That was fine! Better than the last lesson." Then the child starts laughing, often looking triumphantly at his mother. "But I practiced only one day this week!" Since I have experienced the same phenomenon, I say, "Isn't it wonderful how our bodies keep learning after we've done good practice? If you hadn't practiced well, this nice surprise wouldn't have happened!"

The phenomenon of reminiscence, that is, improvement during a period in which there is no practice, is an interesting one which has long fascinated those studying learning. The most frequent explanation has been that some subconscious mental practice goes on in the student even without his knowledge.

Overlearning

Singer (1972) states that overlearning, or practicing past a criterion, results in better retention of that which has been learned. Over-

learning plays an important role in Suzuki's success. Children are asked to review old material again and again, making it a part of them.

There are always points needing attention and each time a piece is reviewed one of these points can be the focus of attention. Because of this we needn't have "irksome uniformity" or "lack of variety" as the dictionary defines boredom. Repetition should always be a vehicle for growth. If the student has reached a high level of performance, he can be asked to "play with all your heart" as one Japanese mother told her child, or "feel the spirit of Bach and Mozart" if he is more advanced.

If parents will think of the necessary repetitions for overlearning as parallel to building a beautiful structure in which every block is the same but the end result is a magnificent monument, there should be anticipation and excitement instead of boredom or tolerance.

To be fully effective, says Oxendine (1968), overlearning must be practiced as seriously as the initial task and with as much attention. Teachers must plan for overlearning. Too often parents and children get the feeling that once you get the hang of it, you can stop practicing. IT IS THE DRILL THAT MAKES HIGH LEVEL PERFORMANCE AUTOMATIC.

"Don't stop practicing a passage until you can play it well three times in succession," Suzuki advises his students. He knows from experience that a task may be learned well as shown by one fine performance, but if the student stops with this, his later retention of the skill will be less than if he practices an additional series of successful trials.

Overlearning often taxes the ingenuity of us parents. Just because a student may have been successful in performing a certain piece does not always mean that he will want to repeat the same piece. Suzuki always asks for the repetitions to be "better tempo, better tone, more musical, better intonation".

Negative Factors Affecting Achievement

It is good to stress the positive factors affecting achievement but negative factors simply cannot be ignored. Gallwey (1977) calls these 'obstacles to learning'. One of the principal obstacles is a poor self-image which spawns all kinds of fears: fear of making a fool of oneself, fear of not being able to learn, fear of not meeting others' expectations. (See the chapter on Self-Image).

The fears that attack the person with a poor self-image are easy to understand. The person who thinks little of himself spends all of his time thinking about himself - what others thought, are thinking, and will think about him and his abilities. How can he be free to think about the task at hand? His fear of making mistakes takes all of his power of concentration. To eliminate this fear we must repeat, again and again, that NOBODY, SIMPLY NOBODY, EVER LEARNS A SKILL WITHOUT MAKING MISTAKES, that WE LEARN PRECISELY FROM OUR MISTAKES. There is no way to grow and learn without mistakes.

Perfectionism

We all know the child or adult who is a perfectionist, constantly frustrated because he or she cannot do things perfectly. A child who approaches his study of a musical instrument with a perfectionist attitude should be prepared by parents and teacher for the realities of learning an instrument or he will experience increasing stress as he strives for perfection.

Teachers often encounter frustration in the bright student who is accustomed to understanding and excelling with little effort, and who easily stays at the top of his class. When this student is confronted with the repetitions necessary for learning to play a musical instrument, he often can't understand why this should be necessary and becomes angry with himself because of his inability to perform perfectly immediately. Fear of making mistakes is common but the perfectionist has an extreme aversion to errors. You must say to this kind of child, "People aren't going to be disappointed in you or dislike you because you can't play a new piece right away. Everybody makes mistakes while they learn."

Children should be taught that all human beings are imperfect and fallible. "We strive to be less fallible," writes Dr. David Burns, "but we don't try or pretend to be perfect." A child can and should enjoy the process of doing something very well, but when his primary goal is perfection, each step can be filled with tension and anxiety.

Fear of Success

A fear that usually does not bother the beginner but may affect a more experienced student is the fear of success. This may sound strange because we think that it is natural for every human being to want to succeed, but it is such a common fear that entire books have been written about it. For some reason a student who has tasted success and has received the reinforcement of remarks like, "He's really got it!", "It's going to be fun to watch how fast she progresses!", may react negatively to all of these encouraging comments. Fear of the added responsibility associated with high achievement seems to be the cause. An ex-performer is occasionally heard to say, "I could have been great if I had practiced."

Gregory, our third child and first son, puzzled us by his reaction to success. When he was ten and had been studying piano for several years, he performed on a recital. Congratulatory comments came from all sides. "You play with such musical feeling and vitality!", "What a delightful performance!", "It's obvious that music is very much a part of you!" I looked on, smiling and enjoying a moment dear to mothers. (Parents are rewarded at these moments for the struggle and heartache that seem to be an inescapable part of parenting.)

Not long afterward Gregory asked if he could study the cello instead of the piano. Since he had been studying piano with me, I thought this might be a good idea. He would be playing an instrument that neither parent could play. This might make him feel more independent.

After a year of successful cello study he participated in an elementary orchestra clinic in our area. The results of the tryouts placed him in the first chair of the cello section.

"Why must everyone in the Starr family play a string instrument or piano?" he questioned a few weeks later. So he dropped the cello and began to study French horn. This continued through his high school years.

After an excellent performance of the Mozart Concerto No. 3 with the orchestra at Suzuki's Institute in Matsumoto, he received

31

encouraging compliments on his fine playing. Later as he prepared to return to Japan to go to college, he told us that he wanted to sell his horn. "If I want to play again later, I'll find another."

I always marveled at the fact that comments we expected to motivate and inspire him turned out to have the opposite effect. Was the challenge missing or was the responsibility too great for a child having two professional musicians as parents?

*   *   *   *   *

Further aspects of the learning process will be discussed in the sections on Practice, Concentration, and Coordination of Mind and Body.

For the things we have to learn before we can do them
We learn by doing them.

Aristotle

Gregor Piatiogorsky, the famous concert cellist, remembered that his always cheerful father played the violin day and night. When Gregor was small his father took him to a symphony concert where he heard a cello for the first time. He had never heard anything so beautiful! He soon had his own make-believe cello—a set of two sticks, a long one for the cello, the short one for the bow—which magically conveyed him into his own world of sound. When he was given a real cello on his seventh birthday, he kept it next to him at meals and beside his bed at night, never letting it out of his sight.

Practice

Parents' Attitude Toward Practice

When we lived in Matsumoto we watched groups of mothers meeting with Suzuki on a regular basis. As we became acquainted with some of the mothers we asked them, "What does Suzuki-sensei talk about in these meetings?"

They laughed. "Always the same things. Answering questions about home practice, giving us suggestions on how to motivate our children, and encouraging us to believe that our children all have high ability."

It was comforting to know that even with Suzuki's thirty-year environment, the problems we all face were of concern to him and the mothers in the Matsumoto program.

In a videotape interview for the Suzuki-Starr tapes, I asked Suzuki, "When you speak of mother-tongue education, you mention the fact that the desire to speak gradually awakens in the baby. Would you please give us some advice on how to motivate the child so that he will practice willingly and eagerly?"

"The mother's attitude is so important", Suzuki replied. "Teachers and mothers should teach with love, and should always try to make learning fun. Mothers should not scold their children. When we wish children to learn something, we must first create a willing attitude and a happy environment."

(A recording of this interview is available on audio cassette tape. See Appendix.)

And so, taking Suzuki's advice as we approach the problem of home practice, we must first look at ourselves and our attitudes. Most of us, if not all, would say that our principal motive was that of enriching the child's life. On the large scale our attitudes can be quite healthy, but on a day-to-day basis, faced with our child's reluctance to practice, we may exhibit far different attitudes.

Shigeki Tanaka, kindergarten director working under Suzuki's guidance, stated, "Since nothing is as important as the beginning, I take plenty of time there. I foster the joy (confidence) and interest (concentration) of doing the simple things everyone can do, more and more skillfully (accurate and fast)."

If we look forward with pleasure to the daily practice sessions with our children, this joy will show in everything we say or do. If we have to learn to feel this way, we should act as though we already do. Didn't William James tell us that an emotion acted out repeatedly becomes our own?

Practice: When, Where, What, How Much

A regular practice schedule is the best for small children. They grow to expect practice every day at the same time. Practice then takes on the quality of inevitability. It becomes part of the routine.

"Where" to practice should be a place that has no aural distractions, and visual distractions should be minimal. If there is likely to be anything distracting outside, the child should not face a window.

Here's an example of "when, where, and what" in our home when Michael was five years old. The time is 7:00 a.m. and the place is the bathroom off our bedroom. I'm shaving and Michael is standing on the commode practicing his newest most difficult passage. He liked to do the hardest part of his practice first. My ears are open and my eyes move his way enough so that he sees that Daddy knows what's going on. Actually, it was my shaving that was on 'automatic' at these times.

I used to delight in his concentration on repetitions of small fragments. I never knew how long each period of concentration would last. It varied every day, but most often Michael did his best work at the very beginning of each morning practice. Judith and Tim took a little longer to warm up but lasted longer.

When Michael seemed to tire, I changed direction, asking him, "Which piece would you like to review first?" I can still picture him, now six feet two, standing on the commode playing Minuet No. 2 with great fervor.

A Japanese mother who was known to be very successful working with her little daughter said, "I left the violin out where Hitomi could reach it. When I heard her pick it up and start to play on it, I appeared quickly and guided her for a few minutes of practice." (I should mention that this was a mother who did not work outside her home and who had only one child.) Hitomi's mother did not regard this as a sacrifice. "I just loved to watch my daughter play. It was a game for me, too." Years later we saw this mother, whose daughter was then a very advanced violinist, watching young beginners with childlike delight.

When I've told this story of Hitomi and her mother, I've had mothers protest, saying, "I've done the same thing, but my son simply wants to scratch on the violin. He doesn't want me to regulate him in any way. When I try to get him to practice the way his teacher asked him to, he won't do it. He just walks away."

My advice was for the mother to say to the child, "I'm glad you want to play the violin. Let's play some games the teacher wants you to do, and then you can play a game of your own", or, "Can you show me the way your teacher asked you to play?"

Length of Practice Periods

Suzuki points out that practice periods should grow along with the span of concentration. "At home two or three minutes of practice may be enough for a beginner. Perhaps this can be done four or five times a day. Gradually each practice period can be longer as the child begins to play the Twinkle Variations. If he can play all the variations of Twinkle, which may take four minutes, his ability to concentrate is also developed to that length of time. As other pieces are added, the period of concentration lengthens naturally".

Psychologists agree that a given amount of practice time distributed over several short sessions, with rest or contrasting activities in between, leads to more learning than the same amount of time spent in continuous practice. Of course, the short sessions have to be long enough to overcome the warm-up period which is generally inefficient. An interesting aspect of separated practice sessions is that errors often disappear during the intervening time but correct responses are retained. Intervening periods also give the child a chance to recover from physical or mental fatigue.

In some instances it has been shown that more skill can be attained from less total practice time if practice time is divided into several short segments. As children become more advanced and are practicing much more, it becomes difficult to find time to create a number of short practice periods. When a long period is unavoidable, it is best if there is contrasting material covered in each session.

Quantity and Quality of Practice

Suzuki often comments on the rapid advancement of the children who practiced well and hard. "A child who practices well shows it in his playing. You can tell immediately. Practicing according to the correct method and practicing as much as possible is the way to acquire ability. If one is faithful to this principle, superior skill develops without fail. If you compare a person who practices five minutes a day with one who practices three hours a day, the difference, even though they both practice daily, is enormous. Those who fail to practice sufficiently fail to acquire ability. Only the effort that is actually expended will bear results. There is no short cut. If a five-minute-a-day person wants to accomplish what the three-hour-a-day person does, it will take him nine years to accomplish what the other does in three months.

"For someone to complain, 'But I studied for five years' means nothing. It all depends on how much he did each day. What a person should have said is, 'I did it for one hundred and fifty hours and I'm still no better.' To put your talent up on the shelf and then say you were born without any is utter nonsense.

"The development of ability is straightforward. People either become experts at doing the right thing, which is seen as a fine talent, or they become experts at doing something that is wrong and unacceptable, which is seen as lack of talent. So it behooves everyone to become expert in the right things, and the more training he receives, the better. Depending upon these two things — the amount and the quality of the practice — superior ability can be produced in anyone."

Most American children don't seem to be spending as much time practicing as their Japanese counterparts. We parents shouldn't lament the fact that our children don't progress as rapidly. We should *accept the hard facts about quantity and quality of practice, and strive to help our children practice as much and as well as possible. Our commitment of time and energy will of course depend upon our family priorities.*

During the last few years Suzuki has been urging students to practice a minimum of two hours a day. I wonder how many families are following this advice. Fourteen years ago when we spent our year in Japan we found that many students in the middle and high school years were thought to be doing well managing one hour a day for practice. Homework assignments took a great amount of their time. Although they were in the minority, one always heard more about the students who were practicing three and four hours a day.

Conditions of Practice

Practice alone is not sufficient for improvement. According to Singer (1972) practice is wasted unless it is accompanied by the student's interest and attention, meaningfulness of the task to the learner, understanding of the goals, intent to learn, readiness to learn, knowledge of results, and a strong relationship of the practice conditions to the performance conditions. Slightly overwhelming, isn't it? If all of these factors were present at practice times, a parent's life would be easy!

In line with the above statement, perhaps it is not too bold to say that no practice between lessons might be superior to poor practice. Mitsumasa Denda said he preferred his beginners not to practice at all between lessons if the mother and child didn't understand what was to be done, or if the child were allowed to practice very badly and get into habits difficult to correct.

"Children learn," Suzuki insists. "They learn either good or bad habits. It is wrong to say that they haven't learned when they play badly. They have learned — they have learned to play badly."

Observers note that children who have bad playing habits are consistent in the application of these habits. They've learned well how to play badly. Watch a child who is holding the violin incorrectly while playing. He always holds it incorrectly in the same manner. He does not shift from one poor playing position to another.

We must realize, however, that students cannot produce perfection as they learn. Current thinking among physiologists (Wilson, 1982) is that we begin to learn to make complicated moves rather laboriously — working out the details step by step, making corrections when we observe our own mistakes, and consciously and deliberately establishing patterns of movements that eventually become less tentative and finally become smooth and sure.

Practice Format and Goals

The child should be given opportunities to express himself about the practice format. This helps foster a responsible attitude toward his practice.

Kyoko used to ask Michael to do certain things ten times a day. In the first practice session I would say, "Let's see, Michael, Kyoko asked you to play this part ten times every day. How many times do you want to do it now?" He often gave a number higher than I expected. If she hadn't requested a specific number of repetitions for a certain passage that we found troublesome, I would ask him how many times he thought it should be played. Again he most often gave a number higher than I had anticipated.

Each practice session should have a goal, even if it seems to the child to be only a number of correct repetitions. Judith, Tim, and Michael all showed expressions of self-satisfaction after completing a number of repetitions, often heaving a sigh of relief for having gone over the hurdle. Children are proud of accomplishments, even small ones.

Most children like to count repetitions. One of the best things Kyoko did for Michael was to ask him to draw the bow straight twenty thousand times. "Twenty thousand!" Michael exlaimed in dismay. "But when you play the last variation of Twinkle once you will have played almost two hundred bowings", Kyoko reassured him. Michael really enjoyed checking off two hundred at a clip. He was delighted to see that five playings gave him one thousand. Twenty thousand didn't seem so far off at all!

As the children got older, we found that it was more difficult to sell them on counting repetitions as a goal. Many teachers have reported that they've had trouble with certain bright youngsters who, after they understood how a passage should be played and then played it well, couldn't see the necessity for repetitions. "I already know how it should be played," one might say. This is where Suzuki's famous saying comes in, "Knowledge is not skill. Knowledge plus ten thousand times is skill!" In later pages we'll discuss how we can aid in making these repetitions not only palatable but enjoyable for our children.

Repetitions of pieces already learned are much more pleasant for the children since the appearance of variable pitch tape recorders. Since the pitch is adjustable to the piano's tuning, beginning pianists can play their first melodies along with the recorded left hand part, while the more advanced pianist may sometimes do the review pieces along with the complete recording. Violinists can play along with accompaniment tapes or the recording itself. Most children enjoy playing straight through pieces with accompaniments. This is a musical experience that seems far removed from practice. I remember watching a small Japanese girl in her home in Matsumoto playing piece after piece with the recording. She looked as though she were imagining herself on a stage performing before a rapt audience!

Sometimes on those "bad days" it's very difficult to get the children to attempt anything new. I remind parents that one can still benefit a great deal from review practice. If you sense that your child, for whatever reason, is too disoriented to practice new material effectively, why don't you suggest the child play a mini-concert just for you? For each piece that is played you can suggest one point to be observed for improvement.

Specific, Reasonably Hard But Attainable Goals

Teachers have the responsibility of establishing goals for the student's lessons, and the parent, the goals for each practice session, although the student should participate in setting particular practice goals. Goals that are specific, and reasonably hard but attainable, will produce much better performance than too easy goals or a general goal to do one's best. "Reasonably hard" is difficult to define. Both the teacher and parent will, by trial and error, become more proficient at guessing what "reasonably hard" goals should be for each particular child.

At a workshop for teachers in Knoxville I brought our eight-year-old Michael to take a lesson on the second violin part of the Bach Double Concerto. I wanted to demonstrate to the teachers an example of a 'specific, reasonably hard but attainable' goal for a single practice session. "Michael always likes to work on the hardest passages first", I explained, "and then coast the rest of the session".

Directing him as a parent would, I guided him through six repetitions of a portion of the difficult c minor passage on the second page, a passage that is usually played quite badly out of tune because of improper practice. I asked Michael to play the 'taka' rhythm on each note. "Place your fingers very carefully as Kyoko asked you to do", I requested.

This passage is thirty-one notes in length, but I asked him to play only the first twelve notes, making sure that his hand was in the proper position before he started each repetition. Then I stopped. Michael had been giving total attention to his work and I wanted to stop while we were both ahead.

I turned to the teachers and said, "I think that was a reasonably hard goal, because I was being so specific about the placement of each finger. It was also attainable because Michael knew it would be short. Didn't you think that was enough on that passage, Michael?"

"It sure was! And you didn't yell at me either!"

Perhaps his remark demonstrated that my goals during practice at home were at times unreasonably hard and evoked tension in him and me. At any rate, it exposed my human frailty as father and home teacher and at the same time strengthened my credibility as one who understood parents' problems.

Kyoko Kawamoto told of asking a small Japanese boy to go over a passage again and again. Since he was doing so well, she kept on and on. "Suddenly he put the violin down and started to scream! I hadn't noticed the tension building up in him. I told myself that in the future I would have to be more observant of the student's feelings."

PRACTICE

Manual Guidance. Knowledge of Alternatives

When Michael was three, I decided to start him on the violin by guiding his bow arm in the 'taka-taka' rhythm one thousand times! I had seen so many beginners bow crookedly that I intended to program him with correct input only. Since he had never done it incorrectly, I thought he would naturally do it correctly when he began to draw the bow by himself. It seemed inevitable that he would fall into the pattern that I had established. (I learned later that psychologists called this "external manipulation of the passive learner".)

When I finally asked Michael to do it himself, I found out how truly passive he had been! His bow wandered all over the place as though he had never moved the bow before! I didn't realize that training by guidance, particularly of a passive learner, may restrict the information offered to the learner by withholding a knowledge of alternatives. According to Holding (1965), "Knowledge of the correct response is incomplete if there is no opportunity to define it against the alternatives. We cannot be said to understand 'red' if we have never identified other colors."

Samuel Belov, one of my teachers at Eastman, said, "You should be wary if, when practicing a difficult new passage, you play it well from the beginning. You will know it better if you can compare your correct and incorrect renditions". At that time I was astonished to hear what I later found was excellent advice.

Good teachers and parental home teachers often show alternatives to students by drawing their attention to the feel of an appropriate movement contrasted with the feel of inappropriate alternatives. A student playing incorrect alternatives occasionally is not learning those errors as long as he knows which response is the correct one.

I said that Michael was truly a passive learner during that period. A strong indication of this passive role came one day when, in the middle of repetitions of 'taka-taka' in which he was totally uninvolved, he released both bow and violin and walked off to do something of his own choice. I made a violent lunge and managed to catch both before they hit the floor! After I recovered, I walked into the living room.

42

"You know", I said to Connie, "since we're leaving for Japan in six months, it's really foolish of me not to delay Michael's study until we get there. That way we can observe first-hand how a Japanese teacher works with a beginning student."

"That's a good idea," she replied. Then she added with a grin, "Was that a sigh of relief I heard?"

Mental Practice

Mental practice works well with older students, but there has to be sufficient prior experience before mental practice becomes valuable. Fritz Kreisler, the famous Austrian violinist, was known to be a master of mental practice. It was said that he could study a new piece from the printed page, then perform it in a recital without ever having played it before! Of course, the idiom and the passage-work must have been very familiar to him.

The use of a mental review following a performance may provide feedback that the performer might not have noticed otherwise. Many performers have said that after a concert they are mentally able to play over an entire performance in explicit detail with very keen aural and kinesthetic images. In fact, some have said that they couldn't avoid playing the program over, that it came to them unbidden!

The great violin pedagogue, Ivan Galamian, taught that mental control over physical movements was paramount in importance. In guiding the technical development of his students, he sought to make the sequence of mental command and physical response as quick and precise as possible.

Mental anticipation of motions to be made and mental reflections on motions made are valuable tools for the student. Suzuki's 'stop-and-prepare' method gives the student ample time to make a mental image of what he is doing before he plays the passage. Mental reflection on a motion just made is more difficult for students but it is very helpful if they can retain, even for only a moment, the feel of a certain motion, whether it was right or wrong.

Aids to Mental Practice

I like to play games like the following with students to develop more sensitivity to mental placement.

"Put your violin up in playing position. Close your eyes. Now move your hand up to third position where the first finger should rest on the note A on the E string. Now before you play the note, can you tell me whether it will be flat, sharp or on target?" If the student is not able to tell me anything at this point, I ask him to play the note and then try to associate the pitch with the distance he moved up the string. I ask him to repeat the process to see if he can improve his judgment of the distance his hand should move.

I use this game for bow placement. "Put your violin in rest position. Close your eyes. Raise your violin into playing position. Now place your bow on the E string at the very middle of the bow. Do you think your bow is straight? Is it in the middle? Is it midway between bridge and fingerboard? Now open your eyes."

If the child has not placed it correctly, I ask him to place it correctly while his eyes are open, then close the eyes and try to be aware of the feel of the hand and arm in the correct position. He should then return the violin to rest position and repeat the whole game.

Even beginners profit by the use of mental preparation before practice or performance. It is an excellent habit to develop.

I use this game for the placement of hands and fingers on the keyboard. "Please put your hands on your thighs in rest position. When I tell you the name of the piece I'd like you to play, find the notes on the keyboard with your eyes only, then tell me the name of the first note in each hand and which finger plays it." I allow enough time here for the student not to feel rushed. "When you are ready, put your fingers on those keys but wait until I say 'ready, play' ". If the child fumbles, we go back to rest position and begin again. The student must be able to place the fingers exactly in position before starting to play.

Another version of the same game may be done with the student's eyes closed. I name the piece, then ask the child to tell me the name of the first note in each hand and the fingers that play those notes. After he does that, I ask him to open his eyes and place his fingers in the correct places.

I use another game for 'listening' mental preparation. "Put your hands in place for 'Go Tell Aunt Rhody'. In your head listen for the beautiful tone you will hear when you play. Think of the tempo that you will play. When you have done this, you are ready to begin."

The New Piece

Some children are so motivated to learn a certain new piece that they will easily agree to practice carefully. These are wonderful times for parents, as are the times when the children review pieces with eagerness. In these cases, motivation is created by the music itself. This is the best, the healthiest kind of motivation.

The desire to play a new piece may not always work out so well. Unfortunately, some children are so impatient to play a new piece that they don't want to take the time to stop and practice it carefully. How wonderful it would be if there were some gadget that prevented the child from making any sound at all if the piece wasn't played well! But again, unfortunately, a child may be able to get through a piece in what may sound like an acceptable manner, but may have incorrect bowings, bad posture, and wrong fingerings. The mother may be so glad to hear the piece played that she may overlook the quality of the performance.

If the child does learn incorrect bowings and fingerings, it's very difficult to undo this learning. I know first-hand how difficult it is to restrain enthusiasm for playing the next piece! We want the child to be motivated by the music itself, and then we're caught putting on the brakes so that the child will learn it properly.

Are you unable to curb your child's enthusiasm to play straight through pieces? (Actually, some parents say they don't like to stop their children because they're afraid they'll suppress their desire to play). If deterring your child seems to cause a great battle, why not say that he can play straight through as a reward for having practiced carefully on certain passages? If it's a review piece, you can tell him to go ahead and play straight through the piece, but you should give him one point to observe and report to you on that point after he finishes.

It is possible to play on the violin what sounds like a creditable performance of Twinkle with a poor bow hold and a poor violin hold. Oftentimes a parent may become annoyed with a teacher, calling the teacher 'too fussy' because of her insistence on correct violin and bow holds. The performance sounds reasonably good to the parent. She may not think the position is all that important since the child can play. It should be understood, however, that a consistent bad posture and bad bow hold will certainly severely limit the child's growth.

I like to show students and parents that I can play a reasonable-sounding version of Twinkle holding the bow in my fist and holding the violin very low with a slumped hand, but that I simply cannot play a reasonable-sounding version of the last movement of the Mendelssohn Concerto with the same poor position.

"See", I exclaimed to one little boy, "When I hold the violin and bow this badly I can still play Twinkle but I can't possibly play this concerto by Mendelssohn. I'm asking you to be careful with the way you hold the violin and bow so that later you'll be able to play all kinds of advanced pieces like this one." My demonstration backfired as he complained, "But I don't want to learn to play that piece! It's way too hard!"

The Terminal Case

Those who have been present at workshops we've given around the country have probably heard the phrase used by Bill to describe students who are allowed to proceed without the necessary attention to basic posture and position. He calls them 'terminal cases'. Although they may be able to give a seemingly acceptable performance of the easy pieces they will never be able to progress through the more advanced literature. Their study has a built-in termination point. When this is understood, it is easier for students and parents to accept the teacher's zealous attention to details.

Parents See the Difference

A teacher told me that one group of her beginning pianists had been quite slow to acquire the necessary basics of the Twinkle variations.

Beth, one of the group, had begun to play very well and progress quickly after almost a year and a half of study. Her posture, hand position and tone were all excellent.

"My husband was transferred to another city so I assigned my students to other teachers in our area. Two weeks after the assignment Beth's mother phoned me. 'I wonder if you could assign us to another teacher. Let me explain why. Yesterday one of Beth's neighborhood friends came to our home. Since we knew that she had been taking Suzuki piano lessons from the teacher you assigned to us, we asked her to play for us. She'd had only a few lessons and she was playing all of the Twinkle variations! Her posture was awful, her hand position terrible, and the tone was not good. Now I know why we stayed on Twinkle so long, although at the time I really wondered whether it was necessary. I can see that Beth has a really solid foundation. She's gained so much confidence because of it, too. We want to continue that way so we hope you can find us a teacher who will work that carefully with us.' I was sorry that I had made a mistake assigning that teacher, but I was delighted to hear that this formerly skeptical mother could see and hear the difference that a slow, careful beginning can make."

Sometimes, through situations like this, it becomes obvious to parents that the teacher's insistence on going 'side-ways' until the seemingly simple habits are acquired is the best insurance for future growth.

Relationship of Practice to Performance

According to a well-established psychological principle, movements practiced slowly will transfer to a rapid continuous performance in direct proportion to the extent that the movements made in performance resemble those of practice. This is not so much of a problem in the early years as it is with advanced students.

A specific problem for violinists is rapid shifting. When they practice these shifts slowly, they must be very careful to practice them with the same motions they will use when they play up to tempo. So many students, when they shift rapidly, adopt a different hand position from the one they used for slow practice. No wonder they are insecure about fast passages!

Judith was always quite attentive to details of practice. I felt comfortable leaving her to do her own repetitions while I looked in on Tim or worked with Michael in the next room. I could hear her carefully going over the passages we had discussed.

As she became more advanced, however, I realized that she needed to become even more aware of what Gallwey calls "increasingly minute muscle and energy sensations in the body". She was working on a passage in thirds. "Judith," I said, "if you're not careful about your arm position here, you can practice this passage over and over again and never feel secure when you play it fast."

At first she was not particular about what she was doing, but after a week or so of practice she realized that she wasn't building up any security. Then she began to observe her arm position carefully. This was a turning point for her. After this, she became increasingly aware of the need for her practice conditions to be as closely related as possible to her conditions of performance.

David was amazed at his freedom and accuracy in the performance of keyboard jumps after I reminded him that during his slow practice he should visualize the jump, pinpoint the target and move slowly and rhythmically in the shape of a rainbow to the second note without stopping *before contact. That last instruction was the most important one. It meant that the practice movements would resemble those of performance. There is no time in most musical performance to stop —* "to be sure" *— before playing the second note of a jump. Logically then, this stop must not be present in practice.*

"That's so much easier!" David said as he demonstrated a jump up to tempo with confidence.

Parents and students who are aware of this important relationship between practice and performance can save much time and frustration during the years of study.

Mother—Assistant Teacher

I often suggest to teachers, in order for them to aid parents as much as possible with home practice, that they make remarks like the following to beginners: "Alice, I'm asking your mother to be my assistant teacher during your home lessons. I'm asking her to write down everything I want you to do at home, and to try to follow my instructions as carefully as she can. It's a great help for me to have your mother's assistance. I expect you to do what she asks at home as carefully as you do for me in my studio."

I've even introduced the mother to the child as home teacher. The children always laugh at this because it seems so absurd to them. "John, I want you to meet Mrs. Brown, my assistant teacher in your home. Oh, I know she's your mother! I just wanted you to be sure to know that she is also my assistant. She's going to do the best job for me that she can. I know that you'll give her the same fine attention you give me. You and I are both lucky to have your mother's help. You'll learn so much easier and faster this way."

You can enlist your teacher's aid in getting your child to practice every day. Suzuki says, "Have your teacher ask your child how he practices at home. If you are trying to get your child to practice before going out to play after school, request your teacher to ask your child to practice every day at that hour before playing and add, 'Mark it down every day you do this, and report back to me at the next lesson'. This can be said quite casually. From this the child will feel a stronger sense of obligation to the teacher."

For beginners it might be helpful not to use the word 'practice' at all. "Let's play the piano for a while". I like the way many Japanese refer to home practice as home lessons. Since the mother has been identified as the assistant teacher at home, this makes sense. It should cause the child to expect the home lesson to resemble the lesson at the teacher's studio. Then the mother could say to the teacher, with the child present, "We are both going to try hard to make our home lessons as good as the lessons here".

Attitude of the Learner

The child should have the intention of improving his performance each time he practices. We should try to convince him that each good practice session adds to the whole. Children often do not believe that when they are in the early stages of a learning situation. They have only a vague feeling about what their practice will accomplish.

"Every little bit of good practice helps you to program your inner computer", you can remind them. "Remember when you couldn't even play 'taka-taka'? Now it's easy for you. After you work hard on a new piece that at first seems really difficult, it will become one of your 'easy' pieces. Try to remember that when you practice."

Child's Attitude Toward Teacher

One of the most powerful factors in motivating a child to practice is the child's desire to please the teacher. You as a parent should take advantage of this by showing your respect for the teacher and cultivating respect for the teacher in your child. The more your child respects and admires his teacher, the more he will want to work for her. I like the way Suzuki puts it: "Accumulate a debt in the child's heart which urges him to practice."

Remarks about the teacher's expectations should be phrased in a positive manner. They should not put the child in the position of having to produce or be a failure. "Mrs. Evans is really happy when you show that you have worked for her. Teachers try not to show it, but they are disappointed when their students don't practice well. If Mrs. Evans knows you've tried your best, even if you make mistakes, she'll be pleased." Children need to understand that teachers are pleased mostly by the efforts of their students.

At a party we staged for them, our students were shown what it's like to be the teacher of a non-cooperative student. They played a few pieces together and then sat down in a circle. An older student, her identity concealed behind a clown's mask and costume, came in for a lesson. "Who wants to give the clown a lesson?" I asked. Little red-haired Monica, all of five years old, rushed forward eagerly. "O.K., Monica. The clown wants you to teach him how to play 'taka-taka stop-stop' on the E string, but first you have to put him in the proper playing position."

Monica pushed and pulled at the clown, adjusting his arms as she kept instructing: "Hold the violin like this under your chin. This is the way you should hold your bow. Don't slump your left hand." She then stepped back to survey her handiwork before she gave the order to start playing. The clown immediately slumped out of position. "No, no," exclaimed Monica, hurrying to set everything right. Again the clown fell into a bad position. Monica's voice rose, "Please hold the violin and bow the way I show you!" After her next adjustment, the clown again slumped out of position. Monica made one more attempt, only to meet with the same response. Suddenly she stamped her foot. "I quit!" she said, turning on her heel and returning to her seat.

If Your Child Loves to Practice

There are some children who fall in love with the violin, even very small children. They will practice for three or four hours a day without any coercion. American parents hearing the Japanese tour group are continually amazed at the very rapid progress these children have made. Here are some revealing quotes from mothers whose children advanced very rapidly at an early age: "A friend played the violin at kindergarten graduation. My daughter came home and said she wanted to play the violin no matter what!" "My nephew enrolled for lessons. Our daughter saw him and insisted on doing it herself." "My daughter saw her friend's lessons and asked and asked to join. She insisted for a month." "My daughter envied the violin of a friend who was taking lessons. She craved the violin so much that a friend gave her a violin as a toy."

When we read of the famous concert artists we often encounter the same stories concerning their early interest in the violin. Several begged for a violin at the age of three.

Supervision of Practice

If our child loves to play so much that there is never any need to urge him to practice, we are fortunate in having most of the battle won. We should rejoice at not having to devote any energy toward motivation, but we still have a great responsibility to see that the practice is worthwhile. The quality of our supervision of practice is critical and can save the child untold hours of remedial work.

Concert violinist Franco Gulli stated, "Each day my father would practice with me one hour. I never practiced the wrong way, and was thus able to achieve much more than the average talented child who struggles by himself."

Elmar Oliveira, a recent winner of the Tchaikowsky Competition, had an older brother who taught him how to practice correctly. Of this he said, "I think it is of vital importance that a young performer have someone to supervise his daily practice. No single thing is more important than the quality of one's practice."

Suzuki declares again and again that his approach is not calculated to produce concert artists, but still the method is closely akin to the approach taken by parents whose children did become famous concert artists, particularly in the involvement of an active parent, relative, or close friend who supervised the daily practice of the very young student. In this regard, it has been said that talent is common but favorable environment is not.

So, whether our child loves to practice or not, we still have the responsibility to see that the practice is fruitful. Higher levels of skill are not reached by mere mindless repetitions or half-hearted performances, Mednick (1964) notes. Monotonous repetition does not increase skill; it seems only to make lower-level performance more automatic, or reinforces mediocrity.

If Your Child Does Not Like to Practice

If your child does not like to practice, all is not lost. Even among the concert artists we find those who admit they were forced to practice when young. Pinchas Zuckerman, one of today's front-rank violinists, said, "My father forced me to practice three to four hours a day. I would much rather have been outside playing."

Nathan Milstein, great Russian violinist, praised his mother for forcing him to play. "I started to play the violin not because I was drawn to it, but because my mother forced me to. I was attracted to music. I wanted to hear it and make it. My mother sensed my affinity and made me practice regularly. Only when I progressed to feel the music itself in my playing did I practice eagerly and willingly."

We have seen the following happen many times. Children are attracted to the Suzuki program when they see other children perform, but when they find that practice is necessary for them to be able to play like the others, their initial enthusiasm often wanes. As they practice and become more proficient, however, their motivation increases.

If we parents feel that motivation always precedes action and wait around until our child is in the mood to practice, he may never learn to play. Dr. David Burns, psychiatrist, in his book "Feeling Good" states that we should not put the cart before the horse. "Motivation does not usually come first, action does. You have to prime the pump. Then you will begin to get motivated and the fluids will flow spontaneously."

So many parents have told us, "After they've gotten started practicing, they really get involved. It's not as difficult to keep them going as it is to get them started." Dr. Burns put it this way: "First comes action, then motivation, which produces more action."

A great majority of the Japanese children who did not like to practice and whose mothers sought help from Suzuki and his teachers, developed their potential quite successfully in spite of this problem.

Suzuki told parents who complained that they had a hard time getting their children to practice, "Don't be the kind of parents who insist on the immediate progress of their child. Relax, with a determination to make your child great. It's all right to be slow. Handle it so your child enjoys it. Try to motivate him so that he will try to improve on his own initiative. If you have difficulties with practice, try to create a change of attitude gradually."

I for one am happy to see how much sympathy Suzuki has for parents who have trouble with their children's practice. He is always optimistic, feeling that sooner or later the child's attitude, as fostered by a loving parent, will change for the better.

Here's an example of the realistic advice he gave a troubled mother whose child would not practice with her. (This is an illustration of the manner in which Suzuki puts the child first, even, in this case, above his own method!) He advised the mother, "Let the boy practice by himself. Say to him, 'Mother will be in the next room listening'. Of course the child practicing by himself will not do so well. You should tell his teacher that you are trying to create a desire to practice, and ask the teacher to show your child how to practice every detail. Wait for your child to ask before you assist him at home."

It is Suzuki's hope in this case that the boy will eventually change his attitude as he realizes that he does much better practicing with his mother's help.

Many parents have found that it is a good idea to announce an approaching practice session so that the child has a chance to wind up whatever he's doing at the moment. We should also alert him not to get involved in something that will take a lot of time and will have to be interrupted by the practice period.

The Stalling Child

What do we do when the child stalls and stalls? If we have enough time, we can ride it out and come out ahead, but what do we do when we have only thirty minutes and our child will not start on time? Suzuki says again and again to his mothers, "Don't scold!" So what do we do? Looking over many years on my successes and failures in handling this kind of situation, I feel that both the child and I were winners when I didn't lose my temper or cause the child to become very angry. An older child may be able to get some effective practice done after an angry exchange, but not a young child. I've seen children practice while their tears flowed, both in Japan and in our home, but I'm not sure much was accomplished during those sessions.

Persistent firmness generally works. The first rule is that the child should not be permitted to do anything else while he is stalling. The staller should be restricted to the practice place. We shouldn't call repeatedly, "Please come to practice now." We noticed that Japanese parents didn't waste a lot of energy calling their children repeatedly. If a small one didn't come right away, the mother went and picked him up.

Teachers or parents who have not experienced this kind of frustrating behavior don't realize how painful it can be. You feel as though you are in a no-win situation. If you press the child too hard, he may break down and get nothing accomplished. On the other hand, if you're too lenient, he may extend the stalling throughout the entire practice session. We've found help in the fact that children who don't want to start practicing also don't enjoy a whole session of sitting at the piano stalling. Most will resign themselves to practice as the lesser of two evils.

I think the important thing for us parents to remember is that we should not sink to immature, childish behavior. We must remind ourselves that our immediate goal is to guide our child through some meaningful practice that we both should enjoy. Even if only ten minutes of the thirty was meaningful practice, we have achieved something. Our son David at times used a highly developed technique of stalling, the kind of stalling that would drive a busy mother crazy! Connie asked me to sit with him at the piano on several of these occasions. I used to feel good about the times I could outwait him, even though he might have settled down to work only during those last ten minutes. Here we should repeat Suzuki's advice: "Try to effect a change of attitude gradually."

Boredom

"Most small children like repetition", Suzuki insists. "It is the adult who shows his boredom or displeasure and communicates it to the child. 'She is bored with this piece', a parent will say, not realizing the influence this remark has on the child's attitude."

I've said this to parents who've remonstrated with me, insisting that that wasn't true in their case, that their children were actually bored while the parents were not. Whatever the cause for their expressions of boredom, I have seen some very young children with a well-developed capacity for boredom, a condition that saddens me.

In order to prevent or lessen boredom in our children, we need to work at it all the time, not just at music practice. We need to help increase our children's awareness of the countless beautiful and interesting things, happenings, and people that surround us throughout life. Remember Robert Louis Stevenson's famous lines:

"The world is so full of a number of things, I'm sure we should all be as happy as kings!"

Young children are naturally open to the wonder of everything in their environment, so when Michael started Montessori school at the age of two and a half, he was fascinated by the shapes he'd learned to recognize at school. Whenever he discovered a triangle, square, or parallelogram in his surroundings he exploded with excitement! I remember that I wore a hound's tooth checked wool skirt one day and as

I walked along with Michael I noticed that he kept looking at my skirt. Suddenly his eyes lit up. "Parallelogram!" he sang out as he pointed to the pattern in the material. Sure enough, there it was—a small but quite distinct parallelogram!

Unfortunately he was not so excited by toilet training. By this time I was not so excited by it either, having lived through three other boys who had helped me to understand that there should be no rush. The job would be accomplished when maturation dictated. . . a little like Suzuki. . . "Provide the environment and wait." So I was encouraging but not pushing Michael in this endeavor.

One summer afternoon during Michael's naptime I was occupied in the kitchen. I perked up my ears when I heard an excited call from the bathroom and ran to share in the joy of his supposed accomplishment. There was Michael—standing in front of the commode. "Look, Mommy, look!" he pointed delightedly at the seat, "an ellipse!"

I remember keenly a trip I made to Atlanta, taking some students to hear Gregorian Chant sung at a Trappist monastery near there. One of the students was a geology major. She kept up a running travelogue as we drove, pointing out to us the changes in the soil and the general topography as we skirted the Smoky Mountains on our way to the plains of Georgia. No one slept. It seemed the shortest trip I had ever made on that familiar road.

Suzuki once said, "When I go in to a room to teach small children, I stop for a moment so that I can descend to their level of physical ability, and can rise to their level of childlike wonder and awe."

Our Privilege

As we help our children with their daily practice, we should remind ourselves that our participation in their growth in music is not an obligation but a privilege and an honor. We should be happy that we have a front row seat for this stage of their learning as we enjoy their daily progress.

I worked extensively with three of our children as they learned to play the violin. Now they are all grown, and as I write these pages, many happy experiences come back to me. The struggles and pain seem much more distant.

We didn't always do the right thing, but then there is no such person, so the psychologists say, as the 'perfect' parent. Neither is there a 'perfect' teacher, or 'perfect' child, and that, of course, boils down to the fact that there is no 'perfect' human being. So no parent should be laden with guilt because he has fallen short of perfection. Still, this doesn't excuse us from trying our best and from making ourselves knowledgeable in all the ways that can help us function as the best parents we can possibly be.

At the foundation of all our efforts must be that most important ingredient—Love. It is love that sees each child as a unique person made in the image and likeness of God. It is love that works to help that individual become all that he can be.

"The greatest good that we can do for others is not just to share our riches with them but to reveal their riches to themselves." Anon.

Additional material on practice will be found in the following chapters on Concentration and Coordination of Mind and Body.

The question is not what you look at
But what you see.

Thoreau

We do not stumble over mountains
but over molehills.

Confucius

The most glorious moments in your life are not the so-called days of success but rather those days where out of dejection and despair you feel rise in you a challenge to life, and the promise of future accomplishments.

Flaubert

Concentration

Webster gives the word 'focus' as the synonym for 'concentrate', calling concentration "directing of the attention, or of the mental faculties, toward a single task or object". From our own personal experience we know that there are different levels of concentration, from merely paying attention to complete absorption.

Directing our attention, or paying attention, requires a certain amount of self-discipline. We have to restrict our sensory input to the object or task at hand. As we become more interested in the object of our concentration, less and less effort is needed to maintain attention. We experience the highest state of concentration when we are totally absorbed in whatever we are doing or observing. It is this last state that is exemplified in superior athletes or superior performers in any field.

We recently heard an interview with the winning Olympic discus thrower, Al Oerter, who has become a legend in his own time. "When I am out there in the event", he said, "I'm not aware of anything around me, the noise, the crowd, or even the place that I am in."

Zen philosophy states it simply this way, "When we sleep, we sleep; when we walk, we walk; when we eat, we eat; when we study, we study."

Japanese Children

On my first visit to Japan with a group of American teachers, all of us marveled at the total absorption that we saw displayed by the young children. Whether they were performing or taking lessons, they gave undivided attention to the task of playing. "What is the secret of their concentration?" we questioned each other. Never had we seen anything like this in children at this early age.

Perhaps the secret is the age-old influence of Zen philosophy on the Japanese culture, an influence that is still nurturing the Japanese children. Experienced observers like John Kendall have commented that the cultural environment as a whole is a strong contributing factor to the marvelous examples of superb concentration shown by the little Suzuki musicians. We came to see the great value Suzuki teachers and parents placed on the ability to concentrate and the persistent efforts they made to help the children achieve it.

Living in Matsumoto with our family, we became part of the society. We saw exceptions to the rule, but came away with the strong impression that many more Japanese children, particularly those in families involved in the Talent Education movement, seemed to be 'centered', or were able to focus more easily and for longer periods of time, than their Western counterparts. This impression has not changed but has been reinforced as we continue to work with children throughout the U.S., and in Canada, Venezuela, Switzerland, England, and Australia.

Many of the Japanese children are adaptable to long periods of concentration and practice, and yet these same children are as childlike and playful as all well-adjusted children should be. They don't go about with long faces or act like miniature adults. We saw no antisocial 'book-wormish' types who were set apart from their contemporaries. American families who've had the opportunity to play host to the tour groups of Japanese children have been delighted to see them behave off-stage merely as happy, carefree children.

In Knoxville in 1970 the entire group visited our home, and recently in 1982 they again visited us in Boulder. They had planned to visit Pike's Peak for a sight-seeing tour on their free day, but snow and ice had forced a cancellation of their plans. Since they had planned a picnic, we suggested that they come to our house in the country, with its open view of the mountains and ample room for the children to play.

When they arrived they scattered in all directions. Some jumped on the trampoline, some picked up frisbees, and others played ping-pong. There was joyous laughter coming from all directions.

Miss Yuko Mori, the senior teacher who led the tour, had insisted that the children bring their violins for a practice session, so after lunch the violins were brought out. They all lined up and, at a signal from Miss Mori, began to play with complete absorption. What a beautiful example of their ability to change focus quickly and completely!

Children Respond to Challenge

We also had a marvelous opportunity to see the children concentrate in an unfamiliar learning situation. Mori-sensei had asked Bill to work with the children on the last movement of the Mendelssohn Concerto which they were playing in unison. He made some suggestions on bowing technique that they adopted and practiced with great intensity. After the half-hour coaching session, he asked if they'd like to play a musical game. They agreed eagerly.

It was a tricky game. A piece was chosen. Each child was assigned one pitch from that piece. They then performed it, with each child playing only her own pitch as it occurred in the melody. It sounds easy, but isn't. Although quite a few mistakes were made, they laughingly kept trying until the piece was finished. When Bill sat down, they clamored for another piece. In spite of errors in the second piece, they kept playing and at the end asked for a third piece! They obviously enjoyed the challenge even though it was difficult.

Developing Attention in Beginners

Capturing the attention of the beginner before going on was considered of vital importance by the Japanese teachers. They told us that some of their beginners came in totally inattentive and that it was only with great persistence that they were able to affect a change in the behavior of those students.

It is our responsibility as teachers and parents to help children with the first step toward concentration, that is, paying attention, by giving them specific instructions to follow.

Haruko Kataoka has often told this story of a four-year-old beginning piano student who was unable to follow her instructions for a correct bow. "Teaching the child to bow correctly is the very first step in developing the ability to listen, to pay attention, and to follow the instructions of the teacher. This boy was unable to bow correctly. Lesson after lesson passed, and still he did not listen and do what I asked him to do. I could not let him begin to study music until he accomplished this first step. How could he learn a much more difficult task if he could not perform this simple one? And so he continued to come for lessons for six months. Then he was finally ready."

When we revisited Matsumoto again in 1973, I questioned Mrs. Kataoka about this student. "He is playing well, although his progress has been somewhat slow", she answered.

I have always marveled at the understanding shown by the mother of this boy. Obviously she respected the teacher's judgment in placing such a high value on the ability to pay attention or she certainly would not have returned week after week to a music lesson that involved no music! Could this incident have occurred in our culture? Do we value such growth enough to persist in nurturing it until it is accomplished? We need to ask these questions of ourselves.

Lesson Environment

Japanese teachers, discussing the environment of the lesson, stated that the behavior of the older children, witnessed by the beginners, was perhaps the strongest positive influence on most of the beginners. This is another illustration of Suzuki's contention that environment is extremely important. "When in Rome . . ."

When I first began teaching, I did most of my teaching in my home studio. I tried to keep material for quiet activities accessible: paper for drawing, crayons and pencils and books, with a low round table that was the center for these activities. At the outset, however, not only did the children talk, but the parents talked out loud to the children and to each other, distracting the student who was being given a lesson.

I firmly but pleasantly made our needs known. "Please don't talk out loud during lessons. When you talk, whisper or speak very quietly. When you take your lesson you will want others to be quiet so that you can concentrate. Try to be as thoughtful of others."

Soon the children were coming in, finding something quiet to do, and settling down until it was their turn to take their lesson. As new students would join us, I rarely had to say anything about this anymore. They would see and feel the quiet environment and conform to it. Similarly, the concentration of the older children on their bows and on their physical and mental preparation for performance set the stage for *the younger children. When the younger ones were required to pay attention to those details, they had precedent for such behavior. Most benefited greatly from it.*

With very small children, one can play suitable games to develop their ability to pay attention to, and carry out, specific instructions. The game of "Simon Says" may be used for this purpose. This game is described in detail at the end of the chapter.

Instructions for preparedness for playing the instrument can be used in this game. These should be specific and should always be given in the same order and with the same words. Such a series of instructions will demonstrate the importance of preparedness to the child. They will also help the child acquire the habit of preparedness. It is good to be firm with the beginner, not allowing her to go on to the following step until the next order is given. Countless times we saw young Japanese children wait for their teacher to say 'hai' (o.k., proceed) before they moved.

Paying attention to short specific instructions is not as difficult as maintaining attention as one performs a piece or practices a passage. We need to help our children develop interest which will sustain their attention for longer periods of time.

Studying and Reporting

Most of us who have had school-age children have read articles or books on "How to Help Your Child Study". Again and again we've seen students urged to question themselves on what they have read. "Read a chapter, then close the book and tell yourself what you've just read" is common advice. Some researchers have said that students profit more from time divided between studying and reporting what they've studied than from time spent exclusively on studying.

We ourselves know from experience how much more careful attention we pay when we know we are going to be asked to repeat what we've just read, heard, or experienced. And yet many of us don't expect to be able to recall things easily after only one viewing or hearing. Take listening to directions, for instance. Don't we, as we listen to complex directions, often give up in the middle because we don't expect to remember them and know we'll have to ask for all of the directions to be repeated? But then, of course, we expect our children, however small, to listen to and remember instructions!

I have had numerous occasions to witness the high abilities for immediate recall demonstrated by elementary school children who were having fun. Our university string quartet gave a great number of concerts in schools. Our concerts followed the same format used by musicians throughout the country until I came across this Suzuki-inspired idea to challenge the children and spur their attention to the highest.

At the beginning of the concert, after introducing the players and demonstrating the instruments, I called out to the children, "When composers write melodies for us, these melodies are like people in a story. They keep coming back. The composer knows we won't remember them if he writes them only once. The pieces we're going to play for you today all have some pretty important melodies. You'll know they're important because you'll hear them again and again.

"We want you to listen carefully for these important musical characters because we're going to play a game with you at the end of the concert. After we finish our program, we're going to play a group of melodies for you. Some of them will come from this concert, others will not. When you hear one you recognize from this concert, yell 'yes!', but if not, yell 'no!'. We know that you all have fine memories and will enjoy this game."

The children's attention was wonderful to observe. At the end of the concert, they filled the hall with 'no!' and 'yes!' invariably at the correct time. Of course for the melodies they had not heard I chose ones that were quite far removed from the ones they had. The teachers said the children really enjoyed the game, and felt quite proud of themselves recalling a theme from a Haydn quartet they'd heard only once.

Capturing Attention of College Students

Having taught college students for over thirty years, I know how many listen to lectures, take notes carefully, but have the attitude "I'll learn this later". I used to call them highly skilled recording secretaries. "Why don't you actively try to remember as much as you can the first time round?" I asked. I assured them they would get better and better at it and that it would save them hours of time.

One day, as I was teaching a music-appreciation class, I decided to let them see what their abilities were for immediate recall. I announced at the beginning of the class, "I am going to give a short talk on the sonata form and its use in sonatas, symphonies, concertos and chamber works. I know that this is all new material, but it hangs together pretty well. Don't take any notes. Just listen closely. Ask questions if you don't understand any points. I'll go over the material several times. At the end of the talk I'll give you a quiz on what I've just covered."

There was a chorus of complaints! "You mean we have to learn this stuff right now? No chance for study or review? What if we can't learn that fast? We've never had to do this before, why now? I just can't do it."

I assured them that I expected all of them to get one hundred percent since they would be paying extraordinary attention and there would be no lapse of time for forgetting! After the students quieted down, there was a remarkable change in their attitude. They listened intently and interrupted frequently with questions. One boy couldn't stand the pressure. I was told later that he was secretly scratching terms down on the cuff of his shirt! I gave the quiz, and they did very well which surprised them but not me. I told them they could count the grade if they wished, that I had no desire to hold anything against those who had remained in a state of shock.

Afterwards, one of the best students in the class came up to say, "What a marvelous experiment! I just realized how many hours I waste each week in my lecture courses. I've been what you called a skilled recording secretary. If I learned more in class, I would need to study less, and then would have more time for bridge!"

Many of the students lingered after class, stating that they hadn't realized how minimal their attention had been and how pleased they were to see how well they had responded to the challenge. None, however, wanted me to repeat that kind of class very often! "We just haven't developed the habit of paying attention that long and that intensely!"

CONCENTRATION

Non-judgmental Observations

Timothy Gallwey, in his superb book "Inner Tennis", makes a great point of dealing with anxiety and boredom, recommending what he calls non-judgmental awareness for motivation to sustain people in practice. He developed a number of very clever ideas designed to keep the player's eye on the ball.

We've been working on a similar train of thought to create and sustain children's interest in repetitious practice.

I question the children to get them in the mood for focusing their minds on various things. I start with external objects in the room. "Let's look at this chair. Notice its color, size, shape, position in the room. Is it heavy? Is it comfortable?" If I'm working with small children I don't keep them looking at the chair for very long. I know there's not much they can observe. I move around the room, selecting several more objects for the same kind of focus.

My next move is to the child's body. "Look at your left hand. Notice its size, its shape, the skin, the bone structure, etc. Now close your eyes. Close your fists tightly, then relax your hand. Notice how different it feels. Now move your mind to your feet. Feel the soles of your feet where they touch the floor."

Youngsters enjoy body awareness even though some of them can't feel or observe anything at the beginning. One shouldn't give up if this happens but just come back to it later.

The goal is to increase the child's powers of observation of what he does and what he feels. We should work to make them interested in this kind of awareness. We ourselves can become fascinated with it — fascinated at how sensitive and observant we can become!

If a student knows that she is going to be asked to report what she has observed, she will be much more observant of what she does than if she had just been asked to play. We need to request specific reports from her, but we don't want these reports to be judgmental . . . "That was good" or "That was bad". If we allow value judgments, they will pre-

dominate and we'll get little or no specific information. We won't know what, if anything, she has observed.

A child who has always been very self-critical will say "That was bad" after a creditable rendition while a child notoriously tolerant of her own errors will say "That was great!" after poor playing. Neither of these comments is worth anything.

Not only should we discourage the child from making value judgments, but we should develop the ability to make simple specific requests. "Watch your bow" infers that the beginner should draw short bow strokes and keep the bow straight. I find it much more effective to request, "Please watch how your bow moves straight and remains between the tapes. If it should happen to move past the tapes, please tell me after you've finished playing whether it moved above or below the tapes".

So many times I have had this request followed by a near-perfect performance. Why? Simply because the student was involved.

Occasionally one encounters a student who will bow far past the tapes, then say to you, "I saw the bow stay within the tapes". I would counter with this: "Oh, I didn't see it quite that way. Would you please play it again and give special attention to the lower tape? Remember, I'm not asking you to play it perfectly. I just wanted to know if you could see what your arm was doing. It may not be doing what you know it should do."

Cindy's Improvement

For weeks five-year-old Cindy had been encouraged and reminded by me at her lessons and by her mother during practice, to keep the first joints of her fingers firm. Nothing seemed to be accomplished. Soon afterward I decided to try observation and feedback at her lesson. I listened and watched her play "Lightly Row", a review piece, with the same collapsed joints and concave fingers that had been obvious for so long. When she finished I said, "Cindy, let's try a new game. I'd like you to play the first line of "Lightly Row" for me again. Watch your fingers as you play. When you finish tell me what you saw. Did your fingers collapse and look like this? (I demonstrated playing with collapsed, concave joints.) Or did they look like this? (I demonstrated with firm slightly curved joints.) Now you can play the first line and tell me what you saw your fingers do . . . did they collapse or did they stay firm?" Cindy proceeded to play, fingers firm and curved slightly throughout the entire line! "What did you see?" I questioned as she finished. "My fingers stayed firm," she answered, beaming. "Right! That was great! Now let's do the second line the same way. Watch your fingers again and tell me what you saw." Line after line was performed with the same firm finger position. Naturally this same sequence had to be repeated again and again during practice at home, the mother always asking for observation and verbal response, but after enough repetitions a good habit was born - in half the time required by the usual persistent reminders!

Tommy's Success

At a workshop I was giving a short lesson to a four-year-old boy who had just completed all of the Twinkle variations. I asked his mother to work with him a few minutes while I watched, after which I intended to make suggestions that I hoped might be helpful.

The little fellow proceeded to play the first variation of Twinkle, quite well I thought, but his bow did keep slipping over the fingerboard. Each time this happened his mother said, "Watch it, Tommy. Your bow's slipping over the fingerboard." He dutifully pulled the bow back without stopping. This happened again and again. It seemed that his mother was talking continuously throughout the performance. After he finished, his mother turned to me and said, "You see the problem we're having. Tommy holds the violin up nicely, his left hand position is good, he plays in tune, his bow strokes are short, he plays quickly with spirit, but he just can't seem to keep the bow midway between the bridge and fingerboard. Please work with him."

I complimented Tommy on the positive aspects of his performance that his mother had just enumerated. "Let's play a game, Tommy. Please play that Twinkle variation again. This time neither your mother nor I will say anything at all to help you. But I'm going to ask you to stop playing if you notice your bow moving out over the fingerboard. Don't play one extra bow stroke. As soon as you see it move, you stop. This way we'll see how well you notice the movement of your bow."

Tommy nodded eagerly and began to play. He finished the whole variation without the bow once sliding over the fingerboard! His mother was both delighted and astonished. Tommy was overjoyed by his success and our joyous reactions.

Later I explained to his mother that I felt that he had not been in the habit of feeling much personal responsibility for his bow's motions. He had been waiting for her to tell him when he was off and then he would move the bow back. This time he was totally responsible yet felt no particular pressure to perform since I had not directed him to keep the bow in the right place but asked him merely to observe its motion. This was easy for him to do. He enjoyed it and did well.

Something similar takes place when we drive a car down the highway. We don't command ourselves, "Stay in the proper lane!" We merely ask our eyes to notice when we start to move out of the lane and to send corrective messages to our hands to move the steering wheel. Have you ever noticed all the tiny motions you keep making with the steering wheel without any conscious thought? You wouldn't do well at all if you consciously took over, telling yourself repeatedly to stay in the lane. Try it some time. You'll be surprised how tense you become. On the other hand, you also wouldn't do well if your eyes didn't notice the car's motion because you were looking at the mountains in the distance. Don't try this.

Once I was working with a college student who was studying the Bach Chaconne. I was trying to help her bring out the bass notes in chordal passages so that the harmonies would be clearly heard. Again and again I asked her to bring out the bass . . . to no avail. She had an ingrained habit of playing chords differently. Finally I thought what I had been doing with my young Suzuki students. "Carol, please play that passage again for me. This time listen to the resonance of the bass notes. Observe the beautiful sonorities produced by the vibrations of the lower strings. Don't pay attention to the upper sounds. Just focus on the rich bass." Even though I expected improvement, I was still astonished by the difference in her playing! I began to realize that adults were no different from small children in this regard.

We parents and teachers should make it a habit of noticing the power of the spoken word. What may seem like a slight difference in wording may produce surprising results.

I can think back on the countless times I said to students, "Watch your bow!" Watching the bow can become very boring to a child. How many keep the eyes on the bow for just a few seconds, then allow the eyes to stare out into space or worse yet look all around the room? Or how many keep watching the bow as it wanders all over the place?

Now I use an entirely different approach that invariably produces much more satisfying results. "Please keep your eye on the bow to see how nicely it stays between the tapes. If for some reason your arm doesn't obey your directions or gets mixed up and the bow moves past the tapes, let me know after you stop exactly what the bow did." This request implies that the bow will move correctly and that if it doesn't, it wasn't the child's fault but a lack of muscular control.

I like to bring the child over to my side so that both of us can observe together how the child's fingers, hands, and arms learn to play. I remember a reading expert saying that some children will not try to learn to read because they do not want to subject themselves to the teacher's power to correct them or to declare them wrong or inferior. The kind of approach I'm suggesting here does not put the child on the spot. It minimizes our power to correct them.

Children like to 'pass the buck' of responsibility as well as we adults do. It's great to hear a child say, "My second finger never wants to go down in the right place", rather than, "I can never play that right." If your child starts with the latter accusation, try to shift her to the first which is less personal. "Your second finger keeps forgetting that it needs to be next to the first in this minuet. I think that's because it's been so friendly with the third finger for so long. Please play that part again. Let's watch that second finger. Maybe if he knows we're watching, he'll remember where he's supposed to go this time."

Asking the child to perform with eyes closed is an effective way to develop body awareness. You might say to your child, "Close your eyes and I will draw the bow straight, keeping it between the tapes. Notice how it feels when I do this. Keep your eyes closed. Now you draw the bow. Did it feel the same? Do you think the bow stayed between the tapes?"

We have found in our teaching that this kind of questioning draws the student from merely paying attention to interested attention and then to the highest state of concentration - that of being totally absorbed in what he is doing. And he is relaxed as he moves through this process. Gallwey says, "Calmness and interest are two of the qualities of mind which make it so easy for a child to learn."

By your careful attention during lessons you will be able to carry out the observation and questioning during practice at home that is directly based on the teacher's assignments. Those details may deal with bowing, posture, finger, hand and arm position, tone, dynamics, rhythm, balance of melody and accompaniment for pianists, keeping eyes focused, etc.

When you first begin such involvement and request the student's own feedback, there will often be no response. If you get that blank look or an "I don't know" answer, your response should be "Oh, I guess you forgot to watch and listen! Let's do it again. This time you'll remember to watch and listen and be able to tell me what you saw and heard." Try not to back down and give an answer unless the child seems to be emotionally upset or looks alarmed by being expected to produce an answer. In that case you might want to pursue another tack and come back to it later. If it does not seem that serious, a good positive encouraging response might be, "Sometimes this is hard to do when you first try, but soon you'll be able to tell me what you saw or heard every time you practice something."

This is such an effective tool for productive practice and maximum learning that the effort expended to accomplish it is far outweighed by the results.

CONCENTRATION

A Game to Develop Attention

Since we are trying to help the young child develop concentration and attention, the game of "Simon Says" is a good one. This may be used as a relaxing interlude during a practice session or preceding practice. Specific requests that relate to the instrument being learned or the hands and fingers as they relate to that instrument can be helpful and can be alternated with general requests.

The parent gives a request for an action which is to be followed only if the request begins with the words "Simon Says. . .". Sample requests might be:

Simon Says . . .

> *hold up your right hand*
> *wiggle your left hand (right hand)*
> *clap your hands three times*
> *wiggle your right hand second finger*
> *touch your thumbs together (second fingers, third fingers, etc.)*
> *turn around*
> *jump up and down four times*

Touch your toes. (This request would not be followed by action because it was not preceded by "Simon Says".)

The object, of course, is not to get caught! This requires attentive listening. It is a good idea to set a certain number of requests that the child can expect. "I will give you ten things to do. I think you can listen so well that you will not get caught. Remember, only do the things if I say "Simon Says" to do them." At the end congratulate her on how well she listened. As the child becomes more attentive the number of commands may be increased.

This game may also be played with a group of children. The child who responds to a request without the "Simon Says" prefix is considered 'out of the game'.

Well done is better
Than well said.

       Benjamin Franklin

    The routine followed by the family of Felix Mendelssohn might seem slightly severe by modern standards. The children rose at five in the morning and began lessons with a tutor immediately after breakfast. For relaxation they read serious books, took lessons in drawing and painting, went for long strenuous rides on horseback, and practiced their music. The siblings plus Felix seemed to thrive on this rigid discipline. They were not docile or cowed by it. They simply used their energies seriously and followed the tradition of the family.

Coordination of Mind & Body

*One clue to the concentration we saw in the Japanese Suzuki child-
ren came when Suzuki referred cryptically to the principle of 'keeping
one point'. "From early times," Suzuki explained to his teachers, "mar-
tial arts teachers have explained how to be relaxed and yet centered,
ready for instantaneous action. At lessons, if we ask students who are
tense in their shoulders and arms to focus strength in the area of their
center of gravity, their 'one point', we will find that their shoulders and
arms relax." Aikido practitioners speak of the center of gravity Suzuki
refers to here as an imaginary point in the person's lower abdomen several inches below the navel.*

*Suzuki also has written that physical ability and mental ability are
correlated. Zen writers state that the mind and body are one, that a
calm mind and clear vision are attained in a quiet body, and that only
the quiet and focussing mind can perceive the ticking of a clock or
produce an exquisite tone on a musical instrument.*

We were given an impressive introductory demonstration of these
ideas quite through serendipity. We were waiting in the Seattle
airport on a pleasant day in July, 1973, about to leave for a month's
return visit to Japan, when an announcement came that our plane's
departure would be delayed for two hours.

Mihoko Hirata, a Suzuki teacher whom we'd met in Japan, had
just introduced us to her husband, an aikido instructor and Suzuki
teacher. We expressed impatience at the delay so Mr. Hirata set out to
entertain us.

"Let me show you something interesting," he said, turning to a
little girl standing next to his wife. "Mari-chan, I want Mr. Starr to
pick you up. Please let him." I reached down and picked her up with
little effort.

"Now, Mari-chan, please come over here. I want to tell you something that I don't want Mr. Starr to hear." He took her a little distance

away and whispered something in her ear. She nodded solemnly and returned to stand in front of me.

"Now please lift her again," he requested. Casually I reached down to pick her up. I was shocked to find that I was unable to lift her at all! I repositioned myself to get a firmer grip around her waist and only then was I able, with considerable effort, to raise her feet off the floor. She seemed to be three times as heavy as before but didn't seem to be resisting me at all!

Mr. Hirata laughed at my consternation. "Mari-chan is a very good student!" The little girl laughed and ran off to tell her mother what she had just done. "What on earth did you tell her to do?" I asked in amazement.

"When I spoke to her the first time, you heard me ask her to let you pick her up. Before you lifted her the second time, I asked her not to resist you but to think of the underside of her feet, to imagine that all the weight of her body was going down through her feet into the earth, and to keep thinking all of her weight down as you were trying to pick her up. Obviously, she did this very well as you did have great trouble in lifting her. This shows the wonderful power of the coordination of the mind and body."

"Let me give you another example using yourself as the model. This is called the 'unbendable arm'. First, extend your arm and tense it, attempting to make it unbendable. Now I'll try to bend it up toward your shoulder."

Hirata then put one hand on my upper arm and with the other hand began to push my forearm up toward my shoulder. My arm trembled violently as I tried my best to keep him from bending it. He bent it anyway in spite of my great effort.

"Now", Hirata instructed, "I will show you how to make your arm unbendable without your using any physical effort, but rather using the coordination of mind and body. Hold your arm out straight as before, but instead of tensing it, imagine that your arm is a water hose through which water is streaming toward a fire in your neighbor's house. As I try to bend your arm as before, don't try to resist me but keep thinking of the fact that the water rushing through your arm is putting out the fire in your neighbor's house."

I conjured up the scene. In my mind I saw the burning house and the water rushing through my arm and suppressing the fire before it could spread. Hirata then tried to bend my arm. It remained straight. Surprisingly, I felt no muscular tension as he applied more and more force to my arm.

"Actually," explained Hirata, "the picture I gave you is the one we use with children. I could have asked you to imagine that the power of your spirit was rushing through your arm and out from your fingertips into limitless space. This would have worked as well, but since this was your first time I wanted to stimulate your imagination as effectively as possible. An experienced student of aikido need only ask his arm to remain straight."

These demonstrations seem almost magical examples of the power engendered in us when the mind and body are coordinated. Together with others we later learned, they make a great impression on children and illustrate the fact that this kind of mind-body coordination can produce almost unbelievable results.

The unbendable arm demonstration is most effective if both of the people involved are of similar strength, but I like to ask the child to be the one with the unbendable arm in order to give her added confidence in her potential. I use Hirata's water-hose picture since children respond well to it. Most of the times I've done this the child maintains an unbendable arm. I apply force very gradually, and usually stop after I've reached the same amount I expended the first time when the child was trying to resist. I compliment the child on the wonderful way her mind and body work together.

Many observers who've not seen this demonstration before simply think that less force is being applied the second time. At this point, I often ask the skeptical observer to try to bend the child's arm. That person can then experience the strange sensation of feeling great strength in the child who shows no apparent exertion. I do have to warn certain skeptics not to apply excessive force on the child's arm, or not to apply force suddenly. Either of these actions could distract the child from her visualization of the water hose and the burning house.

When doing this with an older child, we might try Hirata's alternate suggestion, asking the child to relax completely and then imagine that the power of her spirit is rushing through her arm into endless space. Practitioners of aikido call this 'Extending Ki', a principle of the coordination of mind and body.

Suzuki often uses the term 'life force' in talking about the wonderful potentialities of children. When aikido masters refer to 'Ki', I think of it as related to the life force that Suzuki mentions. In extending one's Ki, one must think and believe that the power of her spirit is being projected outward from herself with a positive and vigorous thrust.

After our encounter with Hirata in the Seattle airport, we invited him to one of our institutes in Knoxville where he accomplished wonders working with the children's postures. He first explained the four basic principles to unify mind and body:

1) Keep one point
2) Relax completely
3) Keep weight underside
4) Extend Ki

He told us that these principles overlapped and that any one of them would suffice. "These are four approaches to the same goal. One may work better for some than the others. Certain individuals may at first need several."

Hirata's success with Brad, a slack teenager, was astonishing. I almost didn't recognize the boy whose renovated posture made him look like Heifetz! At first, Hirata told Brad, "Keep one point. This means to coordinate your mind and body by settling your mind at a single spot in your lower abdomen. Don't tense your abdomen. Just put your mind at your one point, which is your center of gravity a few inches below your navel."

To help him with this, he gave him another principle of Ki. "Put your weight underside, or think all of your weight down." Brad at this time was standing with the violin in rest position. "The weight of all objects naturally falls underside. The only time this is not true with the human body is when it is tense."

A third request followed. "Relax completely. Do this as you continue to stand straight. Many people are confused about the state of relaxation, thinking that the body should be slack. They conceive relaxation as a pleasant and weak state and think that it is necessary to revert to tension when action is required." Hirata later told us that if he had asked Brad to relax first he might have slumped more than usual, but after being instructed to keep his one point and think his weight down, he found that he was already relaxed.

Since Brad had been accustomed to bad posture for some time and had been used to daydreaming while he played, he found himself slipping easily into his old posture as his mind drifted away. He had trouble keeping his one point and thinking his weight down. "I've never thought this way before!" he exclaimed. Hirata had to play a few more games with him before he was able to put his mind in one place and keep it there.

The first game was the unbendable arm which Brad did rather well the first time. Then Hirata directed, "Please walk by me. As you walk, think of something behind you." As he passed, Hirata put out his arm to stop him. He stopped him easily. "Now," he added, "please walk by me again, only this time think about going directly over to that wall at the other side of the room." Again he put out his arm to stop him. This time Brad continued without stopping and actually carried Hirata on with him! "Ah, now you see that you can put your mind where you want it and your body reacts accordingly!"

"Now put your violin and bow in playing position. Keep one point and think all of your weight underside. Your teacher has told you to apply arm weight to the bow to get a big tone. To apply this arm weight without force, think of the underside of your right elbow." Hirata then tried to lift the elbow. It was very heavy.

After doing this preparation routine several times, Brad was finally ready to play. Hirata assured him, "As you play you needn't keep thinking about your one point or your weight down. As long as you are absorbed in your playing, you will be holding your one point and your posture will be good. Being absorbed in your playing means to watch and feel your fingers, hands and arms move, to listen to the music you are playing, to sing along with your playing. There are so many aspects of your playing that can absorb your attention. Go ahead and play the Bach concerto. I will check to see if you remain absorbed in your performance."

After he had played a while, Hirata came up from behind him and pulled backward gently on his right shoulder. He was immovable. "If your mind had left your playing, it would have been easy for me to turn you around by pulling on your shoulder."

Piano students at the institute also benefited from Hirata's instruction. He demonstrated the unbendable arm, and asked them to walk, thinking at first behind them, then ahead.

As each student assumed a sitting position on the piano bench, Hirata would question her, "Are you going to play the piano? Yes? Then you must play the piano and not think about TV, or playing outside, or eating ice cream!" He told them that so many times we play the piano only with our bodies while our minds are thinking thoughts of other things. Then we are not really playing the piano.

He went on to explain about 'keeping one point' and 'thinking weight down'. Postures improved almost immediately. Slouching and slumping positions gave way to firm straight backs that showed no tension. "Now if you keep your thoughts on the music when you play, you will always have a good posture and no one will ever be able to move you off balance. When our minds and bodies work together as partners, we are able to do any task beautifully."

I like to use these exercises in group lessons. I say nothing about the one point to very small children, but rather state the principle, "Think all of your weight down", which seems easier for them to visualize than "think your weight underside". I occasionally embellish this to stimulate the children's imaginations, asking, "Imagine that while you are standing straight, you are getting heavier and heavier, that all of your weight is going down to the soles of your feet and then down into the earth!"

As they stand, I walk around behind them pulling on their right shoulders to see how solid they are. I tell them in advance what I'm going to do, saying, "Don't resist me by pressing back. Just keep thinking your weight down and you'll be solid."

I've asked the parents to watch the children closely as I call out, "Now stop thinking about your weight down and think about going out to lunch or out to play." Parents have repeatedly noticed that many of the children start to move and sway as they change the direction of their minds. When I pull on their right shoulders, I have to be very careful. They can be turned very easily. Some almost fall down.

I practice this with the children before I ask them to play. As they prepare to play, I say, "Please think all of your weight down after you place your violins and bows up in playing position. Think how heavy your bow elbow is. This will help you produce a beautiful tone. When you play, watch and listen to yourself play. Just play the music with all your heart. As you are playing, I'm going to walk around behind each of you and pull backward on your right shoulder. If your mind and heart have left the music, I will be able to turn you around easily."

Children are usually able to remain focussed on their playing for short pieces. If a child complains, "But I don't know what to think about when I play", we must give her specific suggestions that will help her maintain her concentration. We must first train her to watch, feel, and listen to her playing, develop her powers of observation, and her aware-ness of what she is doing.

There is no better example of coordination of mind and body than that demonstrated by an infant totally absorbed in trying to pick up something in her hand for the first time. Coordination of mind and body is always a fascinating thing to see. How enjoyable it is to watch the superb athlete in top form, the great musician producing a beautiful performance, or our own children totally absorbed in their playing!

A Game for Quieting the Mind and Body

Because the quieting of the mind and body are so important for the beginner we might use a version of Montessori's "Silence Game" to accomplish that purpose in a pleasant way. This may be done before practice, when diversion or relaxation is needed during practice, or at any desirable time during the day.

The parent sits in a comfortable, relaxed position and asks the child to assume a similar pose. The comments that are necessary should be brief, quiet and followed by stillness. "I am going to ask you to close your eyes and listen. Listen to the sounds you hear in this room . . . in rooms

80

around us . . . outside. After a while I will quietly ask you to open your eyes very, very slowly, and we will talk about what you heard. Now make yourself comfortable, close your eyes and listen to the quietness and the sounds around you."

At first the time period should be short, then extended to longer periods as the child becomes capable of greater control and quietness.

Actually the parent could use this game in its original form with all siblings in the family. After the same preparation as above, and after the children's eyes are closed, the adult tells them in a whisper that a soft voice will call their name. The parent then moves quietly to a spot behind each child in turn and in a slow, drawn-out manner, calls each one by name. Each child opens his eyes, rises and follows the parent's beckoning gesture walking around the room. This is a kind of meditative experience.

A Game for Body Awareness

Since the children need to know the number names of their fingers as they are used on their particular instrument we can use a finger number game that will also promote body awareness.

Invite the child to hold his hand upright with fingers extended. Touch each finger, saying aloud the number name. (Remember: For violinists the index finger will be 'one', for pianists, the thumb is 'one'. This can be confusing to a child who plays both instruments, a good reason why the lessons on different instruments should not be started at the same time!) If children are quick to identify numbered fingers, invite them to close their eyes, keeping the upright hand in place with fingers still extended. Now softly touch the tip of the finger, quietly asking them to tell you the number of the finger you have touched.

At first this can be done one hand at a time, then with both hands together. Children who know 'right' and 'left' can be questioned by prefacing the number with 'right hand' or 'left hand'.

Doing this requires a physical 'feel' for finger placement as well as concentrated attention.

Talent is a species of vigor.

Hoffer

I dwell in possiblity.

Dickenson

The notes I handle no better than many pianists
But the pauses between the notes —
Ah, that is where the art resides!

Artur Schnabel

Relaxation, Affirmations, Visualizations

Aids to a Positive Mental Attitude

"I think I can, I think I can, I think I can", said The Little Engine That Could. Our children loved that story. We all did. We strained with the little engine and heaved a sigh of relief when it succeeded and went over the top. I hope that story is still around to entertain *and* encourage children. Our oldest children, Kathleen and Teresa, recalled it at the same moment not long ago as we stood near the ruins of the small train station on the top of spectacular Boreas Pass in Colorado. How did that train long ago make that torturous journey over the mountains? In Fairplay, a fascinating, restored Western town, we read an old newspaper account of the train carrying a circus over the mountains through Boreas Pass, just like The Little Engine That Could!

We know that The Little Engine was able to go over the mountain because of its oft-repeated "I think I can", which then became "I thought I could". It visualized itself reaching the top. It kept affirming the possibility of success. Since it could not think two opposing thoughts at the same time, negative thoughts were not possible. It acted as though it were impossible to fail! This is the attitude we should help our children cultivate!

For whatever reason, perhaps it is the human condition, negative thoughts about oneself recur with persistent frequency in many, many people. Suzuki feels that the child learning to play a musical instrument is particularly vulnerable. "Not being able to play is the child's natural condition", he has said. "Since this is so, it often follows that the child thinks he cannot learn to play." We parents, therefore, are confronted with the challenge of helping our children build a healthy, positive mental attitude toward themselves, their potential, and in fact toward all of life.

RELAXATION, AFFIRMATIONS, VISUALIZATIONS

Mind Over Matter

In recent years, much has been written about mental attitudes affecting performance in all areas of life. The sports world is turning more and more to the psychologist to help the athlete. Doctors are becoming more sensitive to the power of imagination in effecting healing. The business world studies means of assisting employees with their mental attitudes. People in all of these areas are finding new ways to help individuals develop, maintain, and strengthen positive mental attitudes. Relaxation techniques, visualization techniques, and the formulation and repeated use of affirmations are finding increased use in these fields. With these techniques it is believed that mental attitudes can be changed by individuals themselves, and as a consequence, they can improve their performance.

Jack Nicklaus's remarks concerning his use of visualizations are well known to golf enthusiasts. He practices these visualizations with careful attention to every minute detail.

Arnold Schwartzenegger states, "As long as the mind can envision the fact that you can do something, you can do it, as long as you believe one hundred per cent. It's mind over matter. The body will follow through. It happens every time I close my eyes before I lift a heavy weight. I imagine it. I do it."

Bonnie Harmon, world champion shooter, declared, "My mental preparation consists primarily of a technique I call 'visualization', a technique consisting of formulating a mental picture of what I want to accomplish."

Betty Wanz, Olympic consultant, describing a self-regulatory program for athletes, writes, "Specific muscle tension-relaxation training is followed by a combination of muscle relaxation, deep-regular-smooth breathing, the use of stimulus words, and imagery. Athletes are asked to concentrate on certain words or phrases by repeating them silently to themselves. Words such as *warm, serene, calm,* and *confident* are used to achieve the desired psychophysiological state".

Richard Suinn, Olympic psychologist, uses what he calls "visuomotor behavior rehearsal" with athletes. "The method can be divided simply into three steps: relaxation, the practice of visualization, and the use of visualization for strengthening psychological or motor skills".

Vernon Ball, world champion backgammon player, prepared his own tape recording of relaxation guides, visualizations, and affirmations. He used it once a day for thirty days prior to his winning the world's backgammon championship.

We could go on and on citing examples of these techniques being used to shape mental attitudes to enhance performance. The tremendous power of the imagination as it affects our behavior and our growth is only beginning to be recognized. Those of us who work with children should become familiar with these techniques. It's not at all difficult for us to learn to guide our children into using these techniques effectively, techniques that we now know are used by athletes all over the world. In a sense, isn't the musician also an athlete? And don't we want to utilize all the aids we can in assisting our children?

Affirmations and Relaxation

Affirmations are positive declarations about one's self or about one's performance of an activity. If repeated often enough while a person is in a relaxed state, affirmations can help build positive attitudes and a sense of self-worth. Properly used, affirmations also effectively erase negative thoughts and feelings.

In order for affirmations to be the most effective, it is necessary for the person saying them to relax the body and quiet the mind before beginning the recitation. Barbara Brown, the biofeedback researcher, states, "To date we have learned that deep relaxation can vastly improve health, but perhaps more challenging is the finding that profound muscle relaxation can lead to startling changes in awareness and states of consciousness."

Richard Suinn, who has worked with Olympic athletes, writes, "I have been extremely impressed by the quality of imagery that is possible after deep muscle relaxation. This imagery is more than visual. It is also tactile, auditory, emotional, and muscular".

Relaxation should always precede the use of affirmations and visualizations. Perhaps the most common relaxation technique used by physical educators and sports psychologists is some form of

RELAXATION, AFFIRMATIONS, VISUALIZATIONS

Edmund Jacobson's progressive muscle relaxation, a procedure they find most effective psychologically and physiologically. Progressive relaxation involves tensing and relaxing various muscle groups throughout the body, one after another.

At Home Relaxation and Affirmations

Below you will find a sample procedure that you may wish to use with your child. Study it and make yourself comfortable with it before you do it together. Naturally, you may make any variations you wish as long as they are in harmony with the goal of the exercise, which is to provide an environment that allows the maximum effect from the use of the affirmations that follow.

You may wish to use the following introductory remarks:

"We're going to do an exercise that will help us to relax our bodies and minds. Many fine athletes do this to help them play better basketball, football, baseball, tennis or golf. This will help you to feel good no matter what you're doing.

"The exercise involves tightening up all of our muscles from toe to head, one part of our body at a time. Then when we relax those muscles we'll know what it feels like to be relaxed. We won't get tired because our muscles are tense all the time. By relaxing all of our muscles we can become calm even when someone or something has made us feel scared or upset. If we have an exam at school, if we're playing a solo on a program, or even if we have an appointment at the dentist, we can still relax and be calm. When we have relaxed all our muscles, our minds will become calm.

"Now, let's begin. First, you may lie down on the floor or sit in a comfortable position." (It is really best for the child to lie down because deep diaphragm breathing is easier and more natural in this position.)

"We're going to take some slow, deep breaths. Picture your chest as a balloon that fills with air when you breathe in and gets flat and empty when you breathe out. This will help. You'll see your stomach push out as you breathe in and then become flat when you empty your lungs of air. If you put your hands on your stomach, your hands should move up and down as you breathe in and out. Let's repeat this slowly a few times . . . breathe in through your nose - breathe out through your mouth, or

86

we sometimes say . . . inhale - exhale . . . that means the same thing."

We're then ready to do our progressive muscle relaxation. Fortunately, children enjoy these exercises. Most do them quite well the very first time.

"Let's close our eyes now and begin to relax our whole body. First, think about your toes and the bones and muscles inside. Tighten your toes. Curl them as tightly as possible. Hold them that way while I count slowly to five . . . 1 - 2 - 3 - 4 - 5. Good. Now relax them completely. Let them go. See how good this feels! (This observation by the child is very important.) We always feel good when we can relax."

In sequence you should continue the same procedure with 1) the feet 2) legs 3) abdomen and lower torso 4) chest and back 5) arms and hands 6) neck and head.

As your child becomes accustomed to this relaxation exercise, she will be able to tense and relax all the muscles at once. The goal is to make the individual really aware of what it means to be relaxed. Many children (and adults, too!) think they are relaxed when they still exhibit tension in a number of muscles. Athletes who have done this progressive relaxation exercise many, many times, eventually can become physically and mentally relaxed within seconds. They bypass the tension portion completely because they know what it is like to be totally relaxed, and they are able to scan their body quickly searching for tension areas.

Now is the time to read the positive affirmations to the child and ask her to repeat them in a very quiet voice.

Below you will find a list of affirmations to use as a guide. Pick and choose those which will fit your situation, and then create your own. Certainly there will be a need to tailor-make affirmations for your unique child and her needs. It is best, perhaps, to use only eight or ten during one session.

Affirmations

1. I like myself.
2. God made me. I am a very special person.
3. There is no one just like me.
4. My body is a wonderful creation.

5. My body takes care of me without my direction.
6. I must eat the right foods, and give my body enough rest so that it will be healthy and strong.
7. I want to learn about the world around me.
8. Music is a wonderful gift from God to all of us.
9. Music makes our lives more beautiful.
10. Music is not 'alive' until it is played.
11. I want to learn to play music on the (piano, violin, cello, etc.)
12. I am thankful that my teacher and parents are helping me to learn to play music on the (piano, violin, cello, etc.)
13. When I play music I bring it "to life."
14. I am thankful for all the great composers who have written beautiful music.
15. To play well I know that I must practice each day.
16. Practice is easy when I want to learn.
17. When I practice well I learn easily and play better and better.
18. Each day as I practice I play better and better.
19. Good practice helps me to enjoy my playing.
20. Before I start to practice I relax and quietly prepare my mind and body to learn.
21. I can relax easily.
22. To relax, I take slow, deep breaths and think quiet, calming thoughts.
23. To relax I think that my body is heavy. I feel all of my weight going down.
24. As I practice I watch and listen to what I am doing.
25. Practicing music trains my arms and fingers to work well.
26. I send clear messages to my arms and fingers when I practice so that they will know what to do.
27. My eyes watch and my ears listen to tell me how to practice correctly.
28. At my lessons I listen to what my teacher asks me to do when I practice at home.
29. I listen to my recordings everyday so that I will know when I play correctly.

30. When I was small and learning to walk I fell down many times and always got up to try again.
31. It is all right to make mistakes as we are learning.
32. We learn from our mistakes.
33. I believe that I can learn easily and well.
34. When I believe that I can do it, I can do anything that I try to do.
35. I have a good memory. It grows better each day as I use it.
36. I remember everything that I learn.
37. I remember easily what my teacher asks me to do.
38. I remember easily all the pieces I have learned.
39. The music I have learned is stored in my mind, and I can remember it whenever I want to.
40. I will be thankful and happy about each new thing I learn.
41. Each time I play music I know I am doing something very important.
42. I give the gift of music to people when I play for them.
43. I can make people happy by playing music for them.
44. I am calm and relaxed when I play for people.
45. I am peaceful and quiet inside and have control of my thoughts and feelings.
46. I thank my teacher for helping me to learn.
47. I thank my parents for everything they do for me, helping me to grow into a fine person.
48. I hope that all children will learn to play music beautifully.
49. I hope that all students and parents will love and enjoy music.
50. I will be kind to everyone.
51. I will do kind, thoughtful things for my family and everyone I meet.
52. I will help to make my home happy by being thoughtful of others.
53. I will try to make others happy, and then I will be happy, too.

After a period of affirmation, ask the child to open her eyes very slowly. It is always best to return slowly to regular activity so that the maximum effect from the affirmations can be realized. At the conclusion of the affirmations, you might say, "Now I'm going to count

*slowly to five. When I say 'five', please open your eyes very slowly.
Stand up and stretch. Now you're all ready to proceed."*

Visualizations

"Visualization", writes Vernon Ball, world backgammon champion, "is nothing more than using your imagination to produce life-like full-color images of your choice on your mental screen."

Suinn suggests that if we visualize a positive goal so vividly as to make it real, and think of it in terms of an accomplished fact, we will also experience winning feelings - self-confidence, courage, and faith that success is attainable. Since we are now aware that the mind does not differentiate between vividly imagined and actual experience, we can develop a powerful imagination as a confidence-building tool! We can create our own experiences of success in our minds.

Children may be guided to do visualizations at home on a regular basis, or some weeks before a scheduled solo performance, preparing them for a pleasant positive experience when they perform. Visualizing the details of an enjoyable performance paves the way for a successful real-life musical experience. This visualization may include the appreciative audience smiling and clapping, the teacher helping the student get ready at the piano, the encouraging pat on the back, the nice sound of the music, the smooth feeling of the piano keys, the well-practiced fingers doing their job with ease.

Again, relaxing and quieting the mind is necessary before visualization, so the relaxation exercise above may be used, or any variation you may find useful. After the relaxation preparation you may, in a quiet, gentle voice, guide the visualization as follows.

"Let's keep our eyes closed and make our own movie inside our head. It will be a movie about us . . . we'll watch ourselves just like in a regular movie except that we will make our own pictures in our imagination. (Pause for a moment, then begin.) Let's walk out the back door. What a beautiful afternoon it is! Is it cold enough for a coat? Yes, even though the sun is warm it is still cold and you're wearing your green jacket over the red shirt and navy corduroy pants that you like so much. You're opening the back door of the car, getting in and scooting to the

other side because Jim is behind you. (If the child plays an instrument that she carries, go through the details of which hand it is carried in and where it is put in the car.) Daddy comes around the car to get in the driver's seat, and I get in next to him."

Now relate details in the environment, and the reactions and feelings surrounding them . . . driving fast or slow, waving to friends in another car, finding close parking space, walking to the building, teacher smiling and greeting students, sitting with parents in the second row, walking to the front, calm and relaxed but excited and eager to play, feeling good inside, bowing, sitting or standing quietly in rest position as you get ready to play, placing fingers on keyboard or putting instrument in position, feeling warm hands, watching fingers move smoothly over the keys or fingerboard, etc., listening to beautiful tone, finishing piece, smiling faces in the audience, teacher saying "Very beautiful".

Go on to add any pleasant details that may be pertinent. This would also be an opportune time to add a few affirmations.

It must be remembered that all of the visualizations must be done in very vivid detail - inner feelings, seeing, hearing, touching, and even smelling should be a part of them. The visualizer should feel as though she is actually going through the experience of performance. The more vivid the imagination the more effective is the visualization.

According to a well-established psychological principle, a skill learned or practiced in one situation will transfer to a new situation in direct proportion to the extent that the new situation resembles the one in which the practice takes place. Fortunately, the mind and nervous system also respond well to visualized performances to the extent that they resemble the real performance. This is the reason why this kind of visualization can be so helpful in preparing the child for actual performance. We have found this to be particularly helpful with adolescents.

Here's an account of visualization being used with surprising results with our son David, then eight. David had been playing piano for three years when he asked if he could study violin, too. We weren't too keen on this since it meant more commitment in an already crowded schedule, but I decided to start him myself. After a few weeks he began to rebel against double practice periods and it was the violin that suffered. He had progressed slowly up past 'Perpetual Motion' when summer arrived, and off I went to a round of workshops. We expected David to keep the piano going through the summer but I decided to let the violin ride and see if he expressed any interest in resuming study in the fall. Nothing was said for weeks after he started school. Then one day, out of the blue, he asked, "Whatever happened to my violin?" And so it was that we got out the violin and prepared for the first lesson in four months. I had been reading about the unusual results obtained through visualization, so I decided to use it with David to see if we could shorten the return to his past playing ability.

"David, let's play a game before you pick up the violin." I then asked him to sit comfortably in a chair and close his eyes. We went through a short form of progressive relaxation of his muscles. We had already done this before, so he was quite capable of doing it quickly.

"Now, David, I want you to go with me on an exciting trip down into your subconscious mind. Right back of your eyes I want you to imagine a heavy door. Open the door, and you will see a flight of ten steps leading to a large room below. Let's count the ten steps as we go down slowly. One, two, etc. . . . Now look around the room. It's filled with computers humming away, and file cases. Those computers are running your heart, your breathing, everything that goes on in your body automatically. Over in those file cases is stored everything you've ever learned. Let's find the file case that says 'music' on it. There . . . the second drawer says 'violin' on it. Open it and find the computer card that says 'Perpetual Motion'. There it is! It has on it all the instructions for your fingers, arms, muscles, and nerves. All of it is recorded in detail. So you don't have to try to remember how to play 'Perpetual Motion'. Your body already knows. You just have to let it play. Put the card in that computer next to the file case. When you go back upstairs, pick up the violin and put the bow on the string. The computer will be directing everything automatically. Let's go back upstairs slowly, and count the steps up as we go."

David opened his eyes shortly after leaving his subconscious mind's room. He picked up the violin, and then proceeded to play

'Perpetual Motion' better than he had before the four month layoff! In fact, the level of performance was so high that Connie, in the next room, thought I was demonstrating for him!

I forgot myself and yelled, "Wow! That was great! I didn't know you'd do it that well! Connie, come and hear David play 'Perpetual Motion' just as though he'd been practicing every day for the last four months!"

Here I made a serious error. I should have shown enthusiasm for his performance, but not so much surprise. After what I told him, didn't we both believe it possible? Anyway, my remarks put David on the spot and broke the magic spell. He played falteringly for Connie. Afterward I wished I had said, "Great, David! That's just what we both expected to happen. It shows what you can do if you trust your mind."

(I'm writing this seven years later. David read it over my shoulder and remembered details that I omitted in this account, among them the fact that the stairs were heavily carpeted!)

Another Form of Relaxation Using Visualization

The following relaxation technique can be used without going through the progressive relaxation sequence if the child possesses a naturally calm and quiet personality, or it may be done after having practiced the progressive relaxation sequence for a period of time with satisfactory results.

Getting the child settled comfortably as before, ask her to breathe slowly and deeply a few times, and then proceed as below.

"I've found a beautiful colored picture of a mountain lake that I want you to see. The water is so blue, so still, there's not even a little ripple in it. Can you see the fluffy white clouds and the bright blue sky reflected on it? Now let's close our eyes and see this picture on a screen like a TV set inside our head. See the lake, the still mirror-like surface, the mountains, the fluffy clouds? Our minds are still and quiet like that lake. Let's say this together: 'I am relaxed, peaceful and quiet. My mind is like that lake, quiet, still and peaceful. (It is best if this can be repeated aloud quietly several times in a kind of sing-song rhythm. Also choose a key word that can be repeated in a quiet voice three to five

times during the relaxation - a word like peaceful, quiet, calm, etc.)

Obviously, you may choose a picture of your own choice, the only prerequisite being that it must conjure up feelings of quietness and calmness. It would be good to change the picture at intervals if you do this regularly.

Relaxation During Practice

"Relax, Mary Ann! You're not even breathing! Put your shoulders down! Relax!"

A well-meaning parent may observe that a child has built up tension during practice and want to help her to release it so that she may practice effectively. Yet we know that a person who is tense cannot be forced to relax by the request or command to "relax". Instead, a few things you might ask your child to do are listed below. You may wish to use all of them or only one as the situation indicates.

1. *Stop for a moment to take a few slow, deep breaths.*
2. *Let the arms hang loosely at the sides. Shake the hands vigorously for about 30 seconds.*
3. *Use the tense-relax method with back, arms and hands.*
4. *Sit quietly, eyes closed, saying aloud two or three times, "I am peaceful and quiet inside and have control of my thoughts and feelings".*

This short but helpful relaxation need not consume a great deal of time, perhaps 5 minutes maximum, but the time is well worth it.

Relaxation Before a Performance

Because I believed so much in the benefits of relaxation, I decided to experiment with my students during the time preceding a solo program. I asked the parents to bring all the students fifteen minutes early and leave them with me. We met in the band room which had a carpet on the floor. The parents returned to the auditorium and seated themselves, saving a seat for their child. I waited until all the children had arrived.

"I'd like you all to sit in a very comfortable position. You may sit on the floor or on a chair. Just be sure you are comfortable enough to stay

*that way for a while without having to move. Now I'd like you to close
your eyes and take a few slow deeps breaths to help you relax and quiet
yourselves." (At this point there were a few giggles and whispers to
which I responded that anyone who did not think they could be quiet
while we did this relaxation could go back to the hall and wait for us. No
one left. I think they were afraid that they'd miss something!) "Ready?
All right . . . breathe in slowly through your nose, then breathe out
slowly through your mouth. Again, breathe in . . . breathe out . . .
Please do this a couple of times by yourself. (I allowed time for them to
do this on their own.)*

*"Now I'm going to read a sentence for you and after I do I will give
you time to repeat it to yourself silently before I read the next sentence.
Just keep your eyes closed, listen to each sentence, and repeat it slowly
to yourself."*

*At this point I chose affirmations from the preceding list. When the
affirmations were completed I proceeded to say, "Now, very, very
slowly open your eyes. We'll walk very quietly into the hall. Find your
parents and sit with them until it's your turn to play."*

*The procession into the hall was amazing. There was almost no
conversation. It was as though they were in a trance. It was obvious
from the performances of the children that they all benefited from the
relaxation and affirmations. They showed poise, centered behavior,
and made no impetuous starts.*

*This group of children ranged in age from five to fifteen. Age seemed
to be of no significance. Afterward, one of the children said, "Mrs.
Starr, I really liked the way you hypnotized us!" Just to alleviate any
parents' fears, I thought I'd better explain what had gone on in our
private sessions behind those closed doors! At any rate, after they heard
the performances the parents indicated they liked it, too.*

Relaxation for Pre-teens and Teens

Michael, from the age of 5, had always been completely relaxed
when he walked onto the stage to perform, acting as though he were
walking down the street with very little on his mind. Until he was
twelve. Then after a performance of "La Folia" he came offstage with
tears in his eyes. "I was so nervous! I couldn't believe it. I've never felt

that way before."

Many parents observe this phenomenon. The age of self-awareness, the painful self-awareness of the growing adult, rears its head during these years, and what before brought no thought of anxiety or fear suddenly takes on a whole series of new feelings.

Previously discussed relaxation, affirmations and visualizations can be used effectively with children this age, with affirmations and visualizations especially appropriate to them. Below are some suggestions. You may add some of your own.

1. I believe in myself, in my ability to grow and learn.
2. I am growing in confidence everyday.
3. My memory continues to improve each day as I am getting older.
4. My ability to play and perform improves as I am growing up.
5. As I grow up, I continue to enjoy playing the (violin, piano, etc.)
6. Each day as I am growing up I practice and play better and better.
7. When I was small, I enjoyed playing for people and I continue to enjoy it now that I am older.
8. I continue to be calm and relaxed when I play for people.
9. Since I am playing more advanced music now, I enjoy practicing and playing more than ever before.
10. While my body is growing and developing I am helping my mind and spirit to grow by learning and playing music.

The principles of aikido may also be used both for this age and for smaller children. These are presented in the chapter on the Coordination of Mind and Body.

Relaxation at Lessons

It was obvious that Mark, age 5, needed some help to be able to settle down during his lesson. His mother and I had discussed his behavior in situations outside of the music lesson - kindergarten, church, and home. She was concerned, as I was, that it seemed difficult for him to be attentive for even a short period of time. We discussed food, the possibility of allergy, and his sleeping habits, without being able to pinpoint the cause of his tension.

Because the family had moved to a nearby town, Mark was forced to change his lesson schedule and he was, for a limited period of time, taking his lesson alone instead of with the group with which he had started. Since he would not be embarrassed by the presence of the other children I decided to try a 'pre-lesson' relaxation.

"Mark, would you please lie down on the floor?"

He looked at me incredulously, "What for?"

"We're going to play a game. Close your eyes, relax and get very comfortable. Put your hands right here." He grinned as I placed his hands on his abdomen. "Now very slowly breathe in through your nose. Breathe in, try to hold it while I count to 5, then let out all the air."

We did this a few times. Then I went through the 'tense-relax' routine, but instead of isolating each part of the body, we tensed the entire body at one time.

"Tense up your body. Tighten up everything - your fists, your shoulders, neck, legs, feet - everything as tight as you can. Tighter! Hold it until I count to 3. 1 - 2 - 3. Now relax. Doesn't that feel great? Just lie there quietly, keeping your eyes closed and enjoying how good it feels. Think of yourself floating on a magic rug - floating, floating through the air."

After a few minutes I suggested, 'Very, very slowly now, open your eyes and stretch. S-t-r-e-t-c-h and then get up. Now we'll get up on the piano bench and begin your lesson."

After that when Mark walked in the door of the studio he'd ask, "Am I going to lie down on the floor again?"

We didn't do that at every lesson, but many times after we'd started a lesson without it I wished that I had taken the time to help him relax. There was definite improvement in his attention and retention when we spent those few minutes on relaxation.

Actually if you feel that your child could benefit from even a shorter version of this before a lesson, you can do this at home before leaving for the lesson or in the car if your schedule is tight. The prone position is helpful but certainly not necessary for a quick, effective relaxation. You might find the list from "Relaxation During Practice" helpful if time is short.

Adult - Parent Affirmations

Thus far we have related the use of relaxation, affirmations and visualizations to your children, who are Suzuki students, but these techniques can be just as helpful to parents in the midst of an active family life. Very few adults can say there is no area in their lives that couldn't use some positive reinforcement. I would tend to be suspicious of the person who did, because most of us have a complex composite of strengths and weaknesses, of confidence and insecurity, of desire for change and inflexibility. After we'd given a talk on these techniques to a group of parents one was heard to say, "Those ideas sound great, but it's hard for me to believe they'd work in my family. I guess I'm too old to change". There is nothing more detrimental to a full life than the feeling that because we are 'adults', we have 'arrived' - that there is no need to go on searching and expanding, or that it is impossible to change 'at our age'. That is my definition of being 'old' - and it can come at age twenty, age eighty . . . or never.

See what the addition of a 'food for the spirit' break can do for you each day.

Here are a few suggestions. You'll be able to formulate your own, unique to your needs. Some of them are the same as the ones given for your children. No offense . . . some needs are universal. Again, we believe that eight or ten of the affirmations at a time will be most helpful.

1. I like myself.
2. Despite my weaknesses and deficiencies, I am a worthwhile person with many good qualitites and valuable assets.
3. I am not a perfect parent. There are no perfect parents!
4. I do not have a perfect child. There are no perfect children.
5. I am a worthwhile (father, mother) who is understanding and capable of intelligent and compassionate parenting.
6. I am always open to new ideas and ways to become a better person, and therefore a more effective parent.
7. I love my children, and I want to show them that love by my actions as well as my words.
8. I will find quality time to spend with my child (children) each day.

9. I will try never to be too busy to listen to what my children want to share with me or talk over with me.

10. When my children want to talk to me about something, I will give them my undivided attention.

11. When my children talk to me, I will remember the importance of eye contact.

12. I will find every opportunity to give a reassuring pat or a spontaneous hug to my children, realizing the importance of physical contact in the expression of my love for them.

13. If I cannot stop my activity to listen when my children come to talk to me, I will explain this if it is not urgent, and make a definite time to listen to them as soon as I'm free.

14. I have confidence in my ability to grow, to reinforce those areas in my personality where I feel inadequate or shaky.

15. When stress and tension make me feel uptight I will stop for a moment to relax, repeating "I am calm" until I regain my composure.

16. I am peaceful and quiet within and have control of my thoughts and emotions.

17. I look at all problems as challenges for which to find solutions.

18. I am excited by new situations and find facing them exhilarating.

19. I like to learn new skills and acquire new knowledge.

20. Learning new skills and acquiring new knowledge helps me to understand the learning process that my children are experiencing.

21. I like to take time to "smell the flowers" and enjoy the beauty of of nature all around us.

22. Life is exciting, and I look forward to each day, wondering what wonderful things will happen today.

23. I greet each day with a thankful heart.

24. I am thankful for my healthy mind and body.

25. I am thankful that I can hear music and the voices of the ones I love.

26. I am thankful for my children, their many gifts and talents and their love.

27. I am happy in my role as a parent. The responsibility is great but the rewards are greater.

28. Working with my child while he learns to play the (violin, piano etc.) is a joy filled time for me.

29. I must always remember that enthusiasm and a sense of humor are the best environment for the enjoyment of learning.
30. I like to help my child relax and enjoy learning to play music.
31. When practice time becomes difficult, I remember to remain calm and keep the proper perspective.
32. I can improve! I can grow! I can change!

Nothing great was ever achieved
Without enthusiasm.

Emerson

The parents of Richard Rodgers, *half of the famous Rodgers and Hammerstein team, loved musical comedy and attended each new one as it made its appearance. The following evenings were spent in their living room singing and playing the entire score from opening to finale. Richard, born in 1902, was exposed to these family concerts from infancy. At four he picked out one finger versions of the songs he heard—at six he taught himself to play with both hands—at ten he made up his own tunes—and at twelve he scarcely left the piano to eat and go to school. In an interview he joyfully said, "What I'm doing today is what I have wanted to do all my life!"*

Motivating The Young Child

"How do you help mothers awaken in their children the desire to play violin?" "How do you help the child to enjoy practicing the violin?" These are questions frequently asked Suzuki in Japan and America. After more than thirty years of experience teaching small children, Suzuki still regards the problem of motivation as *the* principal problem for parents and teachers.

An often overlooked aspect of the mother-tongue education is the awakening of the desire to speak as a result of the environment of the young child. The importance of the role of listening to records for the development of musical sensitivity oftentimes overshadows the effect of listening on motivation. "The baby cannot speak at birth, but in his everyday environment he hears his mother and father speak, and gradually begins his desire to speak," says Suzuki, who tries to follow the same path of motivation in his violin instruction program.

In his book, *Nurtured by Love,* Suzuki describes what he feels is the ideal way to begin instruction:

"Although we accept infants, at first we do not have them play the violin. First, we teach the mother to play one piece so that she will be a good teacher at home. As for the child, we first have him simply listen at home to a record of the piece he will be learning. Children are really educated in the home, so in order that the child will have good posture and practice properly at home, it is necessary for the parent to have first-hand experience. The correct education of the child depends on this. Until the parent can play one piece, the child does not play at all. This principle is very important indeed, because although the parent may want him to do so, the three or four year old child has no desire to learn the violin. The idea is to get the child to say, "I want to play, too", so the first piece is played every day on the phonograph, and in the studio he just watches the other children (and his mother) having their lessons. The proper environment is created for the child. The mother, moreover, both at home and in the studio, plays on a small violin more suited to the child. The child will naturally before long take the violin away from his mother, thinking, "I want to play, too". He knows the tune already. The other children are having fun; he wants to join in the fun. We have caused him to acquire this desire.

"This situation having been created, lessons are led up to in the following order. First the parent asks, "Would you like to play the violin, too?" The answer is "Yes!" "You will practice hard?" "Yes". "All right, let's ask the teacher if you can join in next time". This always succeeds. What a thrill the first private lesson always is! "I did it, too," the child boasts. "Now I can play with the other children". Parents who understand children make fine teachers. In the studio there are private lessons and group lessons. Parents who do not understand children think they are paying for the private lessons and that the group lessons are just recreation periods. So although they make sure that their children attend the private lessons, they often fail to bring them to the group lessons. But the fact is that what the children enjoy most is the group playing. They play with children who are more advanced than they are; the influence is enormous, and is marvelous for their training. This is real talent education".

Suzuki feels that the three-year-old is most desirous of pleasing the mother and therefore regards this as the best starting age. However, by no means all of the mothers wanting to register their children for lessons bring three-year-olds as beginners. "Do you turn older children away?" "What is the oldest child you accept as a beginner?" These questions are often directed to Suzuki. "No age limit", he replies. "I say to mothers of older children, 'Let us start today before the child is older!' "

Although teaching the mother first is generally accepted as being the ideal way for a beginner to start in Talent Education, for one reason or another not all Talent Education teachers do this. Some are content that the mother knows how to teach the child at home. If the child is older than three, the desire to imitate the mother may be overshadowed by the desire to be independent. An any age, Suzuki has found it normal that the child wants to please the parents and teacher. The child expects his parents to be vitally interested in what he is doing, and wants praise for his successful development. In Japan often the whole family shows great interest in the child's violin playing.

When we made a short summer visit to Japan a few years ago I had the opportunity to visit Misako Yanagida and observe piano lessons in her studio. Misako has accompanied the tour group a number of times and is a fine pianist. At the time we lived in Japan she was still a 'kenkyusei'—a student—but on this visit she already had a large class of students in Tokyo.

It was at the lesson of a three-year-old girl, a potential student, that I first saw the effective teaching of a mother and the ideal reactions of the child. Misako sensei was working with the mother, and the small child spent almost the entire time beside the mother's chair, watching intently everything that the mother was doing. She was not just standing there, lost in her own thought. She was obviously aware of and interested in what was happening. It was the perfect example of that 'ideal' way we had heard so much about.

Praise

In a lesson for a beginning three-year-old, Suzuki was heard to say 'umai' (good) after every effort the child made. He never said, "No, that is not good", but only "Good. Can you do this better? Let's try again." He urges the mother also to praise the child at every step. Many mothers withhold praise if the child does badly thinking that if they then praise the child, he will not know when he is doing well and when he isn't. Suzuki explains that there can be degrees of praise and that it is better to be silent than to be critical. In most cases, the ingenious mother can find something worthwhile to call to the child's attention. "That tone was better". "You remembered all the notes." "You held your violin higher". "Your bow hold was good". If the teacher and mother are guiding the child properly they need not worry about a little undeserved praise. "Very good. Can you do better?" is the basic Suzuki formula.

Suzuki is quoted from a videotape interview:

"In Japan, some mothers never say 'very good'. I say to mother, "Please say 'Very good. you can play well, but can you play much better?' 'Yes, I can'. With pieces that are already known, mother and

104

teacher must ask for them again and again asking for better tone, better intonation, and better tempo. Gradually we can make ability from repetition of pieces that are known by the child".

The review of known pieces makes it possible to reach a high level of excellence that is truly deserving of praise and hence is a motivational factor. If the child knows a piece but continues to work to refine it in all ways, a praise response is natural and the student enjoys well-deserved attention.

Attitude of Parent and Teacher

Suzuki was asked about patient perseverance in the mother and teacher. "Patience is not necessary. We don't need patience. While the child is learning to speak his mother-tongue the parent doesn't feel he needs patience. Everyone enjoys the child's learning. My teaching is my leisure time. Children play at lessons. Nice time for children and nice time for mother and teacher. I watch what point I can bring to the child's attention. Patience is not necessary. Mothers should enjoy each step as children learn. Beginners grow so slowly, same as mother-tongue education".

Suzuki is by no means the only teacher in Talent Education who thoroughly enjoys teaching small children. I felt the spirit of enjoyment while watching a number of teachers at work. This spirit was contagious. Many of the children and mothers seemed to be enjoying themselves. Mothers often moved to the rhythm of the music. I was surprised to find mothers of advanced children enjoying the behavior and actions of very small beginners learning 'Twinkle'.

Recently, at a summer institute, a six-year-old girl was performing extremely well in one of the afternoon programs. I was so completely captivated by the actions of her mother who was sitting in the front row that I must admit I didn't give full attention to the performance. The mother was leaning forward, almost out of her seat, extended hands holding a small cassette tape recorder, her body swaying in time to the music, while her beaming face had an almost ecstatic expression! There was no doubt that the child felt those wonderful vibrations that came to her from that spot!—and would certainly feel that music was a glorious part of life!

Home Concerts

Suzuki urges each mother to stage weekly home concerts for the father to be shown the child's progress. These concerts can be scheduled at the beginning of instruction even before the child can perform anything. Many mothers have made this a real event, making small stages or platforms out of boxes for these concerts. At first, the child walks up onto the 'stage' with his violin tucked under his arm and his bow in his hand. After facing the father, he bows solemnly and then leaves the stage. He has shown the father how well he can hold the violin 'at rest'. In the early months when the progress is very slow as the teacher and mother are trying to prepare the child's posture and bow hold properly, the weekly home concert can be quite an incentive for the child. Every small step forward is noticed and applauded.

Private Lessons

Suzuki finds that the private lessons provide a great deal of motivation if the teacher really loves children and enjoys teaching them. The private lesson is always a public affair in Talent Education. Suzuki says that the child should always watch lessons of other children. He considers this environment essential, observing that the child learns from the advanced students possibly more than he does directly from his teacher.

Suzuki expresses considerable sympathy for the teacher just starting a program. "This is so difficult, without the environment of the advanced children to inspire the beginners. When I started in Matsumoto 24 years ago, it was very difficult because of the limited environment of the private lessons. We had at first only six children playing 'Twinkle', taking turns playing on our only small violin! Beginning teachers should expect the beginning year of their program to be the most difficult. Even the second year, their older students will help them teach the new beginners."

In a typical Talent Education private lesson the studio is filled with mothers and children who wait patiently watching private lessons of other students.

"I saw in America", Suzuki commented, "sometimes only one child and one mother alone with the teacher in the studio. This is a very bad environment. Perhaps the child's progress is very slow and the desire to play is very weak. If the mother says, 'You must study', then the child plays only for the mother, not for himself, but if the child sees other children play every week in lessons, he will want to play as they do. Mother and child must stay and watch other children. Advanced children also play in the room. Mothers watch everything. Children enjoy playing for others and enjoy watching others play."

Early Participation in Concerts

Early participation in concerts is a fine motivating force for beginners, Suzuki believes, not only in the home concert, but also in public recitals and concerts. I witnessed a charming demonstration of this idea of early participation at a prefectural concert performed by over four hundred students. Immediately after intermission, members of the audience hurried quickly to their seats to see the beginners bow. The children came on stage solemnly, violins under their right arms and bows clutched in their fingers. After they had been lined up, a chord was played on the piano, and they bowed, staring out at the audience which responded with resounding applause. They then ran happily off the stage. Some had come sixty miles by train for this event!

Concerts and Recitals

Beginners are always taken to concerts and recitals of the more advanced children. They are much more stimulated by the playing of their peers than by adult performances. "In Matsumoto now we have many advanced small children," says Suzuki. "When beginners attend concerts, we find they learn more rapidly than children of the same age years ago before we had such a favorable environment."

Concert deportment is important. The Talent Education concerts in Japan are rather relaxed affairs, obviously given primarily for the children on the stage and in the audience. Children are not kept absolutely quiet throughout the performance. If the mother is always scolding a child, insisting that he not move or make a sound, he will regard the concerts as unpleasant affairs. Naturally, there must be a happy medium. The children cannot be allowed free rein but the atmosphere should not be too repressive. If most of the members of the audience are reasonably attentive, the majority of the children will conform fairly well. Of course, concert behavior is a problem but not one to be solved by the parents forcing 'adult' attention and behavior on a small child. If the child is sufficiently praised for reasonable behavior and attends concerts with some regularity, his deportment will most likely become satisfactory.

Parents should always realize that even a seemingly indifferent child is absorbing more than seems possible. Eiko Suzuki, (no relation to Mr. Suzuki) is one of Suzuki's fine adult students and now a teacher in Talent Education. She began her study of violin at the age of two. Once in her fourth year her parents took her to a violin recital given by a visiting soloist. The little girl did not sit still one minute, but constantly annoyed her father by climbing all over the seat and watching the audience throughout much of the program. The father thought the evening a total loss until several months later when Eiko recognized a sonata being played over the radio as having been on that recital program months earlier. Her incredulous father had to find a concert program to verify her statement before he believed his little daughter who had seemed so inattentive that evening.

Graduation

To increase motivation in the young children, Suzuki has created a system of "graduations" throughout Talent Education in Japan. Talent Education youngsters from all over Japan send tapes to Suzuki to qualify for "graduation" from one level of difficulty to the next. This means that Suzuki listens to approximately one thousand tapes every year. All of the children graduate, and all are rated "excellent" or better by Suzuki!

At the end of the student's selection, Suzuki records comments and advice for improvement. Not all of these remarks deal with technique, tone, or musical sensitivity. For instance, graduates progressing on to the Bach Concerto in A Minor have been given words of advice that must have received warm welcomes in Japanese households.

"Now you are going to play great concertos of Mozart and Bach, and you must try to catch the heart of Bach and Mozart in their music. You must practice every day to catch the feelings of others without words. Look at your mother and father. Can you see how they feel? Try to see when your mother needs your help—before she asks. Then it is too late. If you practice every day, watching not to harm anyone by what you say, and also trying to catch how they feel, then you will develop sensitivity toward the feelings of others. Perhaps later you will also catch the heart of Bach and Mozart in their music."

Suzuki receives many letters from mothers expressing their gratitude to him for these words of advice to their children.

Some Suzuki teachers in the West give pins or certificates to students in recognition of their graduation to another level. These are usually presented at the recital at which the children have performed their graduation pieces.

Institutes and Workshops

Each summer several thousand children are given a heady dose of motivation at numerous institutes being offered in many different localities. The first institute, patterned after Suzuki's summer schools in Japan, was given in 1971 at the University of Wisconsin in Stevens Point, Wisconsin under the direction of Margery Aber. It proved so successful that institutes similar to it began to be offered all over the world where Suzuki music instruction was offered.

Private lessons, group lessons, student and faculty recitals, group, chamber and orchestral concerts, lectures, panel discussions, theory instruction, and related offerings crowd the schedules of most of the institutes. The children are kept busy but at the same time have enjoyable social contact with peers who are interested in musical pursuits. Many parents value this motivation as much as that resulting from the actual instruction involved.

Some families plan their vacations to coincide with institute dates. If all the children in the family are playing instruments and can participate in the program and both mother and father enjoy spending their vacation in this way it can be a great experience. To be that, it must be a unanimous choice . . . everyone must be happy about such a decision.

If you haven't participated in an institute and feel that you could include one in your family vacation plans, ask your teacher about information on institutes in your area or in areas of the country you'd like to visit. You'll be pleasantly surprised by the motivation they provide. Parents have told us that institutes have helped improve the home practice situation for months!

More and more Suzuki programs are offering weekend workshops throughout the school year that are patterned after the week-long summer institutes. Guest faculty are brought in, and sometimes students from adjacent communities are invited. At any rate, these workshops are highly motivational and are also reported to have a salutary effect on home practice. It is not so difficult to fit these workshops into the family schedule, and yet teachers often lament the fact that not enough parents take advantage of these opportunities to stimulate their children musically. It's not that the teachers don't have enough enrollment to finance the workshop; it's that the teachers know how much the children benefit by their participation.

Teacher-Parent Cooperation

The teacher and mother should discuss the problem of motivation together frequently, suggests Suzuki, considering ways to influence the child. The mother and teacher should be very sensitive to the state of mind of the child. Suzuki does not believe that the correct way is to force the child to practice every day. The highest degree of ingenuity and creative imagination must be brought into play to create the most favorable environment for the child.

Happy is he who has the power
To gather wisdom from a flower.

Medieval Saying

Love comforteth like sunshine after rain.

Shakespeare

Although Franz Liszt was not yet big enough for his feet to touch the floor, he would sit at the piano and play all of the melodies that he had heard his father play before him.

Motivating The High School Student

As Suzuki students become older, many parents and teachers become concerned about their continuing Suzuki study throughout high school. The aids to motivation that they have been using don't seem to work as well as when the children were younger. They find that motivating the high school student is quite different from motivating the young student. People are confronted with these questions: How can we make our Suzuki programs more attractive to our high school students? How can we motivate them to continue lessons and practice whether they stay in the Suzuki program or not?

The High School Student in Japan

If we look to Japan for guidance, we find that the structure of Talent Education there provides little motivational impetus for the high school student. Suzuki's program is primarily oriented toward capturing and sustaining the interest of the very young child. We all know with what phenomenal success this has been done. However, the percentage of Suzuki-trained students in Japan who continue to take private lessons and participate in Suzuki concert and recital programs throughout high school is not large.

I was once accosted in Japan by an American teacher who was disturbed by this fact. "Why doesn't Suzuki concern himself more with the older student?" he asked. "What can he do?" was my response. I then explained that most Suzuki students come from families who are not only interested in their children's Suzuki music education but also have a great deal of interest in their children's academic achievements. Many of these parents want their children to attend college.

In Japan entrance into college is extremely competitive. And this competition starts early. Middle school students must pass tests to

112

enter the regional high school which prepares them for college entrance examinations. These high school exams require a great deal of study, consequently limiting or eliminating time for practice.

This pressure causes many of the students to stop taking lessons. Others continue with less and less time allocated to practice. Those who continue studying and do maintain a rigorous practice schedule are the minority who are very advanced and are orientated toward a performance career or are planning to become Suzuki teachers.

The fact that there are so few outlets for performance in orchestra, solo, or chamber music also contributes to a lessening of interest. There are hardly any orchestras in school or college. String players are not motivated to continue repeating the Suzuki literature in group concerts year after year. We saw evidence of this when we noticed, in big group lessons, some of the high school students we knew slipping out of the hall when they reached the easier pieces.

I don't think that thoughts of regret cross the minds of many of these students or their parents. I met a young man who had been a member of Suzuki's original tour group and who was then studying medicine. "Do you play the violin anymore?" I asked. "No," he replied. "Do you wish you could?" "Not really, but I did enjoy it very much when I was a boy. It was a wonderful education for me."

I really think that many Japanese parents feel that their children's education via Suzuki instruction can come to a natural close as their children enter high school. They see the mission accomplished. Recalling the following words of Suzuki, they feel that they have fulfilled an important parental obligation toward their children's total education: "The greatest duty and joy given to us adults is the privilege of developing our children's potentialities and of educating desirable human beings with beautiful harmonious minds and high sensitivity. I believe sensitivity and love toward music and art are very important things to all people whether they are politicians, scientists, businessmen or laborers. They are the things that make our lives rich."

Western Teachers Look Ahead

Teachers and parents in other countries are reluctant to see their students drop out in their high school years. They want the children to participate in music in high school and they see a great number of opportunities for performance available to adults who are skilled amateurs. Youth, college, and community orchestras are open to string players of ability, and opportunities for chamber music also exist.

I have come to know first-hand the regrets felt by many college students who had dropped their study of a musical instrument in earlier years. During the period in which I taught music appreciation to college students, I accumulated over three thousand responses to questionnaires regarding their own musical training and background. Well over half of these students indicated that they had studied music as a child, had disliked practicing, had quit studying and then later had found themselves wishing very strongly that they could play a musical instrument. They also wished that their parents had had the fortitude to keep them at it!

Interestingly, a similar reaction comes from Japan in this story told by a Japanese mother. Her son had been a Suzuki student for a number of years. When he reached the age of thirteen, his complaints about practice rose to such heights that his parents allowed him to quit studying the violin.

Some years later, at college in Nagoya, he roomed with a boy who played cello in the college orchestra (one of the few such groups outside of the music schools in Japan). He went with his roommate to several rehearsals during which the orchestra was practicing Brahms' First Symphony. Captivated by the music of Brahms, he wished that he were playing in the orchestra. At home on a school holiday, he accosted his mother. "I used to play the violin when I was a little boy. Why didn't I continue taking lessons?" "You don't remember?" his astonished mother replied. "You behaved so badly when we asked you to practice that we gave in to your wishes and let you drop the violin." The mother could scarcely believe his following retort: "You should have known better than to have paid attention to a thirteen-year-old!"

Last year during a teacher-training session in Memphis one of the young participants told her own story after we discussed the subject of parents forcing their children to continue the study of music. She said that during her early high school years she told her parents she wanted to stop studying piano. They agreed that when she finished high school that would be fine but until then they wanted her to continue. "After that I became really excited about music and—well—here I am, studying to make a career of playing and teaching." It was a great testimony! As in Bill's story, our children don't always really want us to take their requests seriously. That's what so hard about being a parent—knowing when to stand fast and when to give in!

How to Make Our Suzuki Program More Attractive to the High School Student

First of all, the group lesson itself can provide motivation IF its format is tailored especially for these students. It should not involve much repetitive playing of the Suzuki literature but should reflect innovative programming. Included might be: 1) sight-reading training 2) study of orchestral techniques 3) solo presentations 4) study of advanced techniques not covered in the Suzuki literature 5) learning fiddle tunes and popular songs to be played as solos or in groups for entertainment.

If it is not possible to have a group lesson of this kind especially for high school students, those students should be excused from regular attendance at group lessons. If your child does not attend group lessons regularly for this reason, he should be expected to participate in important group concerts and in recitals as soloist. If he is relucant to cooperate, you should point out to him that he is fortunate to be in a position to give something back to a program from which he has received so much.

Suzuki programs need high school students as role models for the younger children. Both the younger students and their parents are excited and motivated by hearing the older advanced students perform solos in recital. And what a thrill it is to a small group of children who have been rehearsing the Fiocco "Allegro" in group lessons to have five high school students join them at the concert to perform this piece!

Solo Repertoire Can Motivate

More variety in the music given the high school student can make his practice more enjoyable. Short solos that he can play in church or at social functions will be attractive to learn.

Most of the music in the Suzuki books is drawn from the Baroque and Classical periods of music. Music from the Romantic period is usually greeted with open arms at this time.

Parents have heard that the Suzuki literature provides too limited training for students who want to progress into very advanced solo literature, or who want to become skilled orchestral or chamber players. Most teachers in the West have found this to be true, and are supplementing the advanced Suzuki pieces with scales, etudes, reading material, orchestral excerpts, and solos drawn from periods other than those covered in the Suzuki books. As I point out in the chapter, "Orchestral Experience", be sure your teacher is giving your child practical experience in reading music. Etudes are fine for this purpose.

Broadening the solo horizon with a variety of styles of music is one way of stimulating the pianist's interest. There are those who are satisfied by getting into the romantic idiom. Others are excited about ragtime or musical comedy. Jazz interest can grow out of chordal knowledge from theory study and can result in easy jazz improvisation and playing by ear. There are numerous possibilities. Discuss them with your teacher and your child. It's a kind of uncharted course, but can provide some exciting new interests in the same field!

The Strolling Violinist

A number of our students in Knoxville learned a group of popular pieces to prepare themselves for opportunities to appear as strolling violinists. Several of them were able to earn money playing for parties, receptions, and at restaurants.

The students enjoyed the attention they received when performing, but especially so when it came from their peers! Two of them played for several banquets at their high school and were always well received. They were able to play some of the Suzuki pieces as well as the more conventional dinner music selections.

Our son, Tim, began to play weekends at the Hyatt Regency Hotel when he was fifteen. He and a friend who played accordion performed there together for three years. They had memorized about a dozen songs before they auditioned for the job, and kept adding songs that were requested by the diners.

Incidentally, the song most frequently requested was "Somewhere My Love" from "Dr. Zhivago". I arranged a harmonized version for a group of our Suzuki students to close an evening program they gave at a local country club. They brought down the house playing it with the rhythm section of the dance band. The club showed its appreciation by donating a large sum to our scholarship fund.

Orchestras and Ensembles

Students' participation in orchestras generally provides excellent motivation to continue playing, but doesn't necessarily induce home practice on the solo lesson material. Teachers should use the orchestra music to develop the student's technique. (You will find more on orchestras in the chapter, "Orchestral Experience".)

Students who play in a small ensemble with some of their friends find this a delightful experience. Ask your teacher's help in starting a small ensemble in which your child can play. Duos, trios, and quartets often find places to perform. It's nice to see students enjoying sharing these musical experiences with their friends.

We talk about duets, trios, all kinds of chamber music in the reading chapter. Reading is, of course, a prerequisite for this kind of enjoyment. It's true that the music can be 'worked out' but the reading ability decides whether it is more a chore or an enjoyable experience. Developing the reading skill is also a side-benefit of ensemble playing but, paradoxically, an elementary reading facility is required to motivate further action along these lines.

117

Opportunities for the pianist to work with others is limited, so it is very important to pursue and encourage students in this area. There is valuable social enjoyment but there is also the growth of ability to listen and fit with other parts—a sensitivity that is often undeveloped in the pianist who hasn't had the opportunity to spread his wings this way. A new feeling of excitement often accompanies this new experience and with it the desire to explore more!

There are numerous institutes that are incorporating chamber music for teens into their schedules. Look into that for your pianists if you're attending one.

The Pianist as an Accompanist

The pianist can be in great demand as an accompanist as soon as reading ability is established, and he shows that he is sensitive to what goes on in the solo spot.

Opportunities are numerous. The Suzuki pianist can accompany other Suzuki instrumentalists or instrumentalists outside of the fold. There are always choral groups in schools that welcome competent accompanists. Sunday school classes are another outlet. I, and some of my contemporaries, started doing this at a very young age and continued all through high school.

Although an accompanist is usually considered in a background role, if he is capable he will have much enjoyment and a definite feeling of being needed! He may even be able to earn money from his services—a definite motivational source!

Attendance at Concerts of Artists

Live performances by outstanding performers can have a tremendous impact on students. I was a late beginner, starting my study of the violin as I turned thirteen. After a year and a half of study I had the marvelous opportunity of hearing the celebrated American violinist, Albert Spalding, in recital at Bethany College in nearby Lindsborg, Kansas.

My father got us front row seats. I still remember the magic of that afternoon! Spalding's beautiful tone, with his marvelously expressive vibrato, enthralled me! I ran back at intermission and knocked on the door of his dressing room. "Excuse me for bothering you, Mr. Spalding," I hurried to say, "but I'm trying to develop my vibrato. I'm learning so much watching and listening to you today that I wondered if you would please play the slow movement of the Bruch Concerto so that I would have more opportunity to observe your vibrato. It's so beautiful!"

Spalding was very kind. He didn't think my suggestion was appropriate for an encore but he did choose a slow piece to play, and afterwords encouraged me in my work.

I took home, in my head, a sound movie of his playing and played it again and again as I worked on my vibrato. My teacher, for whom the violin was a second instrument, was delighted for me to have this aid.

Today, with so many families having videocassette players, many parents are recording performances by concert artists for their children to see again and again. Researchers in sports have found that people perform better after watching an expert in action. We parents should give our children opportunities to hear both live performances and those on TV. These performances both motivate and teach our children.

During my high school years I remember being as enamoured of the great concert pianists I heard in almost the same way as many kids today are about rock stars! (Well, I guess that's a bit of an exaggeration—I didn't do any crying, swooning, or fainting at the sight of them!) I did cut out publicity clippings I found in the newspaper and kept a scrapbook of programs, autographs, tickets and paraphenalia related to them. And why shouldn't the teen-age tendency to give adulation to the famous be channeled to these representatives of classical music?

Actually there are instances where a few concert artists have captivated the collective public eye. Van Cliburn, when he won the Tschaikowsky piano competition, became a kind of idol. Eugene Fodor, who like Van Cliburn is young and handsome, has attracted a youthful following not otherwise too interested in classical music. Itzhak Perlman is widely known because of his articulate charm. These people's lives are accessible to the young musician of today because of TV and

*other media coverage. Why not encourage a kind of involvement that
makes classical music more alive and pertinent to young lives?*

Solo Appearances

Parents and teachers should work with the student to find opportunities for performance. Numerous occasions for me to perform as soloist in my hometown of Concordia, Kansas provided me with strong motivation to practice during my high school years. I played often at churches, local clubs, banquets, high school functions, hospitals and nursing homes. During my last three years of high school, I averaged over thirty performances per year. Although I was never paid—those were the last years of the depression—I felt fortunate to have that many opportunities to play in public. Kind expressions of gratitude from many people gave me the feeling that I was really contributing a service to the community.

I'll never forget my first performance on our high school assembly program. A freshman, I was clad in knickers that had gone out of style but were hand-me-downs from an older brother! ("They're in perfectly good condition," my mother insisted.) The students of the high school in our town had not had much contact with classical music. I was apprehensive about their reception, but my teacher assured me they would enjoy my playing.

That was an afternoon of shocks. My first shock came when I looked around the curtain and saw the hall crowded with noisy students, with the football team sprawled in the front rows! I almost had to be pushed out on stage.

Fortunately, my teacher had given me a piece (a Sarabande whose composer I've forgotten) that she thought would have an immediate appeal because of its bravura style. It began with several dramatic chords. After the polite applause, I took a deep breath and said to myself, "I'm really going to sock into this!"

The second shock came after my final chord. The students broke into tumultuous applause accompanied by shouts and whistles! I had greatly underestimated my audience, an audience that welcomed me back again and again throughout those four years. I was able to play all kinds of music for them, even solo Bach! The enthusiastic support of those students remains with me today almost half a century later.

These performances in high school included my shortest solo, a performance of approximately one minute in length! I was playing on the commencement program, with my younger sister Virginia at the piano. We had played only a half minute or so when I heard her fumbling with the familiar accompaniment. Glancing over my shoulder, I saw her point to her music. The entire four-page middle section of the piano part was missing! Only the first and last pages were on the piano. I could see my part at the top of the last page so I slipped into that passage and on we went for another thirty seconds or so. Then it was over! I'm sure the audience was astonished by the brevity of that rendition!

Like Bill, I did a lot of performing during high school years— church, school, and clubs. In small towns, clubs are always looking for free entertainment. The fact that it was gratis didn't affect my feeling of importance one bit.

I even had a somewhat regular schedule of personal appearances. Our next door neighbor loved music. He played a bit himself. Whenever they entertained guests I would be summoned to come and play for them.

When kids of high school age are given the chance to perform often for appreciative audiences they realize that what they are doing is not just between them and their instrument. Their skill has a social value. It is an appreciated contribution to the enjoyment of others.

Setting the Stage for Continued Study

If we have been nurturing independence in our children for some time, assisting them to develop their powers of observation and to become fascinated with the learning process that unfolds within them, we have done the best we can to prepare them for continuing study on their own. If they enjoy both practice and performance, the battle is won. No matter how much parents encourage, persuade, cajole, bribe or force their teenager to practice, ultimately the student must want to continue if he is to keep playing. And his desire to play must be strong enough to overcome the pressures of school work and of other interests that may arise.

Some parents, when faced with children who want to quit, make a pact with them to continue study until they finish high school, hoping that, once over that hurdle, they will continue into adulthood. In fact, it is easier for all concerned if this pact is made in earlier years before the commitment is felt so keenly by the student!

All is Not Lost if They Quit

Even if you are not able to keep your children playing their instruments, don't feel that those years of study were a waste of time. Reflect on Suzuki's words addressed to Japanese parents quoted earlier in this chapter. And when you read the chapter, "Life-Enriching Benefits of Suzuki Study", you will notice that you and your children have already shared many of these benefits even if they decide not to continue their study.

During high school years Japanese students who are not interested in a career in music usually do terminate their study. And, as Bill has said, few of them seem to have any regrets.

The important thing to realize is that most of them had been able to develop their talent to a high degree before they stopped. That is quite different from the student who has barely skimmed the surface in his study.

Perhaps we might try to view accomplishments with a different perspective. In a particular period of time we may work hard on a specific skill with seriousness and strong intent of purpose, developing it to a high degree, after which it can be continued as an avocational or 'side' activity. Then another goal may be given first place in time and effort until it has reached the level where it also can be considered functional. I think it is the word 'quit' that sounds like a final loss of some kind. Actually, it is only the termination of active study. For the person who has used that study well the benefits will continue to enrich the life of which it was a part—for a lifetime.

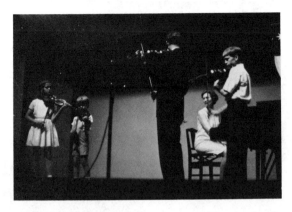

Judith, Michael, Bill, Connie, and Tim in family
performance on stage of Shiminkan in Matsumoto.

Judith, Bill, Jr., and Michael in performance at Stevens Point.

(Photo by Montzka.)

Teresa and Kathleen in the tokonoma (place of beauty) of our first Matsumoto house.

Greg with Yamashita-sensei's baby.

Dr. Suzuki and Tim at Dr. Suzuki's birthday party in the Talent Education Institute in Matsumoto. Hiroko Iritani Driver is in the background.

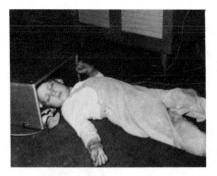

Timmy asleep with the detachable speaker over his head — probably listening (?) to Mahler!

Michael, Greg, David, Bill, and Bill, Jr., walking from Shiminkan to Talent Education Kaikan.

Posted announcement of Suzuki's students in recital, in the basement of the Talent Education Institute in Matsumoto.

Japanese classmate with Michael in the Talent Education Kindergarten in Matsumoto.

Greg in background, David, and Kaoru Tomita after Christmas dinner in our Matsumoto home.

Judith and Bill, Jr., with the display of family shoes in the entry hall of our home in Matsumoto.

In heaven it is always autumn
His mercies are ever in their maturity.

John Donne

The famous Hungarian pianist and composer, Bela Bartok, tells of hearing his mother's piano playing during his infancy. His mother noticed that one particular piece caught his interest and he sat nodding his head and smiling even though he was one year and a half. Soon after he took her to the piano and shook his head 'no' until she repeated that same piece again. By the time he was four he played forty songs by memory.

Listening

As is evident from everything Suzuki has written or said about Talent Education, an underlying principle is that the child's musical education, insofar as the development of his ear is concerned, should parallel the manner in which he acquired his mother tongue. Young children have an uncanny aptitude for recognizing and later reproducing delicate nuances of spoken languages. Suzuki believes and has demonstrated through his teaching that a young child can develop, in the same manner, a highly discriminating musical ear. Much repetitive listening is necessary, just as it is in the acquisition of the mother tongue.

Suzuki feels that the child's musical education should start shortly after birth, with the baby being exposed to repeated playings of a single selection of music. In his *Outline of Talent Education Method*, he writes: "If I let a newborn baby listen to classical music, for example, a Brandenburg Concerto or Tschaikowsky Serenade or a Beethoven quartet, I choose one movement from such classics and let the baby listen to the same tune every day. In about five months time the baby will memorize this melody. If you do not believe this, please try it yourself.

"It is very easy to test whether the infant has memorized the melody or not. To relate one of my experiences: A certain friend of ours had a baby. At that time its sister was six years old and she would practice the first movement of Vivaldi's G Minor Concerto every day. I visited their home when the baby was five months old. The baby was in a good mood and in its mother's arms. So I decided on the test. I played Bach's Minuetto. The baby looked happy. In between I switched to the first movement of Vivaldi, which the baby was always hearing. At the first three notes, the baby moved his whole body in time with the music and looked much happier. He clearly distinguished these two melodies.

"We should try to let babies listen to good music and to nurture a good music sense as early as possible.

"Let me here explain how a nightingale is trained to sing well. If we catch a very young, wild nightingale in the spring and put a good-voiced nightingale beside it for about 30 days, the throat of the baby nightingale changes so that it will be able to sing like its teacher. By changing the surroundings, the wild bird will change in order to fit the new situation. If we use a gramophone to train a nightingale, the bird will sing accordingly—even imitating the sound of the needle going over the surface of the record.

"Almost the same may be said of human beings. Children listen to the pronouncing of words by their parents and their vocal chords adjust themselves physiologically to make the same kind of pronunciation as their parents. The pronunciation of English by a Japanese child and an American child is different. This is because the physical adjustment has not been made by the Japanese child.

"To give a bad example: If a nightingale that sings poorly is kept close to a young nightingale for some time, the young bird will learn to sing poorly. This is one basic rule.

"From my tests of twenty years, I have found that young children who have been given a chance to listen to good music acquire a good sense of music—just like naturally being accustomed to their mother tongue. We should realize that even a child of six has been receiving education for six years. From a musical point of view, the child can be educated by good music, bad music, or no music at all."

When — How

Listening should be established as a daily habit. The child need not be forced to sit down and listen to the recording. He can listen while doing something else. The child easily absorbs the sounds without seeming to be paying any attention to the music. In spite of the fact that Suzuki constantly preaches the importance of much listening, he still finds it difficult to convince some mothers. He remarks that the most effective statement he can make and one that does seem to impress mothers is that THE YOUNG CHILD'S RATE OF PROGRESS IS DIRECTLY DEPENDENT UPON THE AMOUNT OF LISTENING HE DOES. Many students who have been exposed to saturation listening learn new music almost automatically. Their fingers seem to find the right notes without thought.

Some Japanese mothers combine music listening with daily breakfast, and others play recordings as the child lies in bed before going to sleep. Mothers who find that mechanical problems are often the biggest hindrance to the establishment of a daily routine make tape recordings of the song with several repetitions on the tape. Thus they can play a single tape without having the interminable changes that call them from their work. Some use "endless" cassette tapes that repeat continuously. One ingenious mother made a cassette tape recording, then strapped a small cassette recorder to the back of her little girl who then was able to listen while playing in the sandbox in the garden!

The child should not only listen to recordings of the pieces that he is studying, but also to recordings of the pieces that he will study in the future. Some parents make tapes of a whole book of selections which include future works and review. An advanced student may enjoy listening to the earlier pieces for review to help him keep them in his memory for group lessons and concerts.

It is very important that the more advanced student listen to the new pieces well in advance of his study of these pieces. This will save him and the teacher much time as he learns new pieces. One Talent Education teacher asked his students to listen to the Seitz Concerto #5, in Book IV, for six months before starting to learn to play the piece. These same students then played this Seitz movement well after only two weeks of practice.

Adults should understand, Suzuki warns, that the child will not tire of the recordings as an adult might. The small child loves familiar sounds, but if he hears a parent complain about the repetitions of the recording, he may adopt the attitude of the parent and his musical training will be stunted.

Joy of Listening

Long before we encountered Suzuki, we found that our children did not tire of hearing familiar music, and I don't mean just nursery songs which they loved to hear again and again when they were very small. As we introduced them to new music, they often would take a fancy to one particular selection and listen to it hundreds of times. We let them use the phonograph and records themselves, asking them to be reasonably careful. They did take care, but the records were nonetheless worn out. That didn't bother us, because we saw the children making the music their own.

When Gregory and Teresa were four and five, I brought home a recording of Schubert songs sung beautifully by Gerard Souzay. I wanted them to know this wonderful music, so I chose the 'Erl King' to introduce these songs to them. This is a dramatic song about a sick child being carried by his father on horseback while death appears to him as a ghost.

It became a great favorite of theirs. They listened to it so many times they memorized the entire German text. One day Connie heard them singing it together as they rode around and around outside on the whirligig.

They were also drawn to some of the other songs but not to that extent. Gregory liked 'The Wanderer' because of the uplifting change in the music at the end when the disconsolate wanderer recalls his homeland with great joy. In fact, Gregory used to place the needle near the end of the song so he would hear only the change to the bright ending! "I just want to hear the part where he gets happy," Greg explained.

They all used music for jumping. Kathleen rode for many hours on her wooden red horse to the music of the 'Nutcracker Suite', and Timmy and Judith practically wore out a couch jumping up and down in rhythm to the last movement of Schubert's C Major Symphony. I tried to suggest another piece in the same tempo. "No, Daddy! We want this record again!"

We ended up by getting phonographs for the bedrooms. The phonograph in Timmy's room had detachable speakers, one of which he placed over his head 'to get close to the music'. He looked like a creature from outer space lying there with Tchaikowsky's Piano Concerto pouring out of his head! Or the Mahler Fourth Symphony which was another favorite at that time.

When I picked Timmy up at kindergarten at noon one day, he excitedly told me that the teacher had asked them to bring their favorite record the following day for "Show and Tell". "And I'm going to take my Mahler!" I gulped - this was one of those moments of decision. We were so happy that he loved this music. How could we tell him that there was a possibility that this might not be acceptable? We decided to say nothing.

Timmy took the record for three days, reporting each day when he came home, "The teacher didn't have time." He finally gave up. We tried to ease his hurt by murmuring about its length and the lack of time.

Looking back as more experienced parents, we feel that we should have accompanied Timmy to school the day he took the record, explained his love of this music to the teacher, and offered to talk about the music to the other children — a kind of mini-music appreciation class for mini-listeners. In this way, we could have given Timmy our loving support and at the same time possibly opened a musical door for the other children.

Need for Listening Continues

Listening to the recordings of the literature remains important throughout the training of the child. The advanced student may have to listen quite carefully to distinguish the delicate nuances in a performance of a selection such as the second movement of the Bach Concerto in A Minor. Some childen listen to such recordings with the music before them.

Advanced students should be encouraged to listen to several recordings of the same work by different artists. They will find it intriguing to hear the variety in interpretations, although they are often surprised that artists' conceptions of a work may differ widely. We should ask them which performance they like and why. This should make them more keenly aware of the elements that make a superior performance. It should also make them more mindful of their own playing and help them develop a healthy musical sensitivity.

Many of the Japanese homes are quite small, and so the mother hears the recording as often as the child. This makes her role as assistant teacher easier as she is well equipped to help the child because she knows exactly how the piece should sound, and can easily tell when her child is playing a wrong note or playing out of tune.

In summation, Suzuki believes that not only will the child's ear be well trained by listening, but that he will be motivated to want to play the music he hears. Also, the student who has all the music memorized will be able to give all of his attention to the problems of playing the instrument. He will not be distracted by reading notes or trying to recall the next note. Suzuki thinks it is invaluable for the child to develop his musical memory, and to become accustomed to performing without notes.

Parents need to fill a child's bucket of self-esteem so high that the rest of the world can't poke enough holes in it to drain it dry.

Price

The sweetest of all sounds is praise.

Xenophon

To love anyone is to hope in him always. From the moment at which we begin to judge anyone, to limit our confidence in him, from the moment at which we identify— pigeon-hole—him, and so reduce him to that identity, we cease to love him, and he ceases to be able to become better. We must dare to love in a world that does not know how to love.

Anonymous

The Lesson:
Before, During, After

The Boy Scout motto, "Be Prepared", speaks succinctly of the value of preparation in any activity. We could also quote a few Starr versions of proverbs that support the same premise: "An ounce of preparation is worth a pound of remedial work"... "One piece in the head is worth two on the page"... "Where there's practice, there's hope"... "All's well that is worked out well"... "When all else fails, practice".

The First Lesson

Psychologists tell us that we can save the child apprehension and discomfiture by preparing her for new experiences. Even adults are apprehensive when faced with a totally new situation. It helps so much to be familiar with some aspects of the new experience. For this reason it is good for the parent and child to observe lessons of other children for some time before actually beginning their own lessons.

"This afternoon we are going to visit a music teacher who will be giving some boys and girls piano lessons", mother tells Sally. "We're going to sit quietly and listen. If you want to ask or tell me something, please whisper so that we don't disturb the lessons of the other children. You may take a coloring book and crayons or one of your other books to look at quietly while we are there".

In this way the child may observe without any pressure. She learns that quietness is expected and she absorbs the mood of the environment. When she is ready to go for her own first lesson, she will be at home in the studio.

Practice

The first and most important preparation for the lesson is good practice of the assigned material. Naturally the student is going to look forward to her lesson if she feels confident in her practice and is eager to

131

share her accomplishment with her teacher. Everyone enjoys doing a task for which she has prepared with both time and effort. There is the pride and joy of feeling, "I can do this very well".

Most children don't volunteer for practice. I can remember an idealistic soul enthusiastically approaching me with, "Oh, it must be wonderful to be in your family! I can just imagine your children coming to your bedside in the mornings, saying, 'Please, Mommy and Daddy, may we practice now?' Oh, it must be wonderful?" I didn't have the heart to congratulate this lady on her fertile imagination. I'm glad she never had to face reality with a visit to our home! She would have been disillusioned.

There are isolated cases where this kind of thing might happen, however. I know, because I happened to be that kind of child myself. I had decided quite early in life that I wanted to be a pianist, much to the displeasure of a businesslike great uncle who tried his best to discourage me from such an unrealistic and impractical endeavor. I had very romantic ideas about sacrifice and achievement, and I decided that I would get up each morning at five or five-thirty to practice. The house was cold and it was dark outside. These were wonderful props supporting my sacrificial feeling. There was no doubt in my mind that I would become a great concert pianist. . . . Wasn't I suffering like the great musicians I'd read about? I practiced each morning until seven o'clock and then prepared for school. I actually loved to practice!

I was too young to be sensitive to the fact that since the grand piano was at the foot of the stairs, the sound must have been loud and clear in the bedrooms on the second floor. Although my parents and grandparents rose at six o'clock, they never did more than make feeble attempts to suggest a later time for my practice: "Couldn't you wait to start practicing at six?". . . "Aren't you too cold to practice?". . . "You could wait until Daddy fires the furnace at six".

This went on for years. Can you imagine their last hour of morning sleep being interrupted all during that time? In retrospect I am grateful for their tolerance and encouragement.

Although most children don't volunteer for practice, most also don't like to go to lessons unprepared. If circumstances have prevented your child from normal practice for that week, explain to the teacher that she hasn't practiced because:

1. You couldn't work with her because you were too busy.
2. She was too busy at school, or with sports activities, or drama.
3. You had house guests.

Explanations can eliminate grief for all of you. The child will be less fearful of exposing her unpreparedness to the teacher's scrutiny. She can feel that he will understand and not be too displeased by her lack of progress.

If she hasn't practiced because she refused to do so, inform the teacher before the lesson, preferably by telephone, certainly not in front of the child. You will want to enlist your teacher's aid in helping you with the problems.

Daily Practice Record

Keeping a daily practice record is a great non-judgmental tool, especially with the reluctant student. Both the parent and child benefit from seeing just how much time is *really* spent in practice. At the same time, the record provides an objective, non-verbal report to the teacher. He can immediately evaluate the child's work and be more helpful with his guidance. It's easy to understand why a child is not progressing if her practice is minimal. If she is practicing what should be an adequate amount of time and is still not moving at a normal pace, she may need help in learning how to practice efficiently and effectively. If the teacher is knowledgeable about the student's practice habits, he can give her that help.

Relaxation and Quiet Time

Running in from a high-powered game of soccer, Jason heard the screech of brakes as Mom turned into the driveway. She had worried during the whole trip home that she wouldn't make it in time for Jason's violin lesson. Now he was whisked into a tension-filled car for the hurried trip to the music studio. No parking place! (The bane of Suzuki mothers!) "Get out and run in while I find a place to park. We're late! Run!", mother screamed. Thus Jason entered the studio with less than normal composure.

There are days when such a scenario may be unavoidable. We've all had them. But planning and preparation should be done to reduce the number of these occurrences. There is no chance that a child can do her best work under that kind of tension. How much better it is to plan for the lesson in the following manner.

After a short shopping trip, mother picks up Judy at the door of her school. She knows that if she picks her up on music lesson days instead of letting her ride the bus, they will have time for a snack and short relaxation period before leaving for the lesson. "After you've washed your hands, come and have an apple, peanut butter sandwich and milk", mother says as they walk into the house. Following the snack, there is time for a short relaxation, affirmation, or visualization session. With plenty of time to spare, they leave home for the trip to the teacher's studio. They find a parking place and go in without any feeling of hurry.

It's obvious that Judy is in a position to gain more from her lesson than Jason. Preparing and planning ahead for the pre-lesson time yields a worthwhile result. You will see the difference and so will the teacher!

Snack Time or Snafu Time

In this book's chapter on nutrition, we talk about the effect that poor food choices for pre-lesson snacks can have on the quality of the lesson. We won't go into that again here except to say that it is extremely important that parents take this seriously, and many do. Enough is known about the effect of certain foods (or perhaps we should say non-foods) on the behavior and personality of the human being to make us think about and evaluate our own eating habits. We should ask this question: "Do our eating habits contribute constructively to the health of our minds and bodies?" With that in mind, we should choose our foods accordingly. Foods should build health, not just satisfy taste buds.

Enjoy Your Child's Learning

"This is Tuesday! You have a piano lesson this afternoon, Tammy. I just love Tuesdays for that reason, don't you? It's such a joy for me to

hear you play, and I like to hear the other children play, too. Don't you just love Mr. Bridges? He's always so cheerful and helpful. He really shows how much he loves music. You know, when I go to your lessons I forget about anything that's bothering me. I just relax and listen. It's like a short vacation for me."

Compare this scene with the following one.

"Oh, no! This is Tuesday! Jeff, you're supposed to have your piano lesson today. I don't have time to do that! How will I ever manage to get everything done today when I have to spend all that time taking you and sitting through your lesson? I wish you could go on alone, but your teacher insists I have to be there. What a burden! I wish we could skip this week. I don't see what harm it would do. Well, I guess I'll just have to manage it. What a mess!"

Children will respond to joy or resentment, and their own values and attitudes will be formed from that input. It isn't hard to know which of the above children will value and enjoy his or her music learning, is it? Suzuki again and again urges his mothers in Japan to enjoy all of the steps of their child's learning. "The mother should enjoy, then the child will also enjoy."

Don't Put Your Child on the Spot

Doug was a very conscientious seven-year-old. In fact, I had the feeling that he was putting too much pressure on himself, and because of that I tried to ease the burden by not being too demanding of him. Unfortunately, his mother was not aware of this. She had stars in her eyes about his future and tended to push too intensely. Arriving for a lesson, Doug would bow and settle himself on the bench while his mother would say, "Now Doug, show Mrs. Starr how well you can play that piece you practiced so hard this week. Play it just like you did at home. Mrs. Starr, you should have heard him! It was just beautiful. he can really play it. Show her, Doug, show Mrs. Starr how much you accomplished this week!"

And then, guess what happened! . . . Doug's performance sounded as though he hadn't practiced at all! With the pressure to 'show' what a great performance he could give, he crumbled. Heralding too high expectations may place too much responsibility on the child's shoulders. He may fear that he can't live up to them.

Not all children will respond this way, but it's always best not to put any child on the spot to produce. Every child wants to do well, but he may want to give up if he feels that adults around him are expecting too much from him and that he has a good chance of failing.

If a child knows he has practiced well he will be anxious to show the teacher what he's accomplished. Let that incentive carry him through. There may be no need of other reinforcement.

Respect For the Teacher

Your child will benefit greatly from your obvious respect for her teacher, and she should understand why you have that respect. As a skilled professional who is dedicated, knowledgeable, and interested in each student, a good teacher is deserving of respect. The more highly regarded the teacher is in your child's eyes, the easier it will be for you to help her carry out the teacher's instructions. You have a lot to gain by helping to nurture respect for the teacher in your child.

If at any time you cannot sincerely feel this way toward a teacher, it is best to change your situation. Your feelings will speak loudly to the child and to the teacher. No good work can be done in that situation. Choose your teacher carefully and then back him one hundred per cent!

During the Lesson

Teachers like parents to remember these points concerning lessons:

FIRST. Give the lesson your undivided attention. No needlework, no magazines or books to read, and no letters to write, please. If you must bring a younger sibling who is constantly expecting your attention, try to enlist the aid of some of the other parents in attendance to watch him during your child's lesson. If that is unsatisfactory, it would be best to find someone with whom you could leave him for a short time. Of course, if he or she plays well alone and doesn't distract you during your child's lesson, by all means bring him along. You're giving him a head start with listening and absorbing the lesson environment.

SECOND. Bring a notebook in which to write the teacher's assignment and comments, or bring a casette tape recorder and record the lesson. If you do the latter you will have an accurate record of the entire lesson to refer to during the week. It will eliminate any argument about what the teacher said or didn't say. Any question on the assignment can be settled by referring to the tape.

THIRD. Remember that during lessons "silence is golden". We teachers often want to remind mothers that they have the children all week but we have them for only one short period of time. It really is very difficult for a child to get suggestions or directions from two people at the same time. "Whom shall I listen to?" wonders the child. In the case of the piano student, I always feel as though he's squeezed between parent and teacher and can certainly feel pressure when both are giving him instructions. I know how difficult it is to keep from making comments or inserting a suggestion now and then, but it is best to leave this to the teacher at lesson time. Your child will function better and so will the teacher.

FOURTH. Be aware that negative body language is as disturbing as spoken comments. Your child's mistakes may trigger all kinds of body responses you may not be aware of. You may shift position in your chair, take a deep breath, sigh, shuffle your feet, or fold your arms. Any of these tell the child that you noticed her error, are disturbed, or disapprove of what she's done. If this is a regular occurrence the child will soon be more attentive to your actions than to her work, waiting for your response to every mistake.

Many times we can eliminate our negative behavior by just becoming aware of what we're doing. Recently, David commented on my tone of voice. He said that my voice tended to change, becoming tense and tight, when I gave him a lesson or supervised some of his practice. I realized he was right and am trying to catch myself when I hear this happening. I've asked him to tell me if he notices a change at any time during our work together. It should be possible for me to eliminate this fault with his help.

FIFTH. Do ask questions of your teacher if you need clarification of anything that transpires during the lesson. This is one time that talking is not only permissible, it is encouraged! Don't worry about appearing ignorant. Only smart people question what they don't understand. Any good teacher will welcome the interest you show by questioning, so question away!

After the Lesson

Your reactions and comments after the lesson can be very helpful to your child. This is a very good time to review what happened during the lesson. Asking pertinent questions of the student helps you to determine how observant and attentive he was. If you do this regularly, your child will be motivated to observe well and remember what she observed so that she can talk about it with you. This need not take on the appearance of an inquisition, but can be done in a casual manner with you inserting comments and observations of your own. The discussion should certainly not be too detailed or involved so that the child feels intimidated.

Most of all, I am delighted when I hear a parent comment positively on anything that can qualify for praise, whether it be paying attention, listening and trying to do what the teacher asks, being respectful of the teacher, or being pleasant and cooperative. If the time after lessons is remembered as happy and supportive, the student will want to return for more. Pleasant conditioning like this places music study in an atmosphere of joy.

The principle of perfect parenting is simple to express
Err, and err, and err again, but less, and less, and less.
                                                    Piet Heim

Dreary, rainy days
    Children screaming everywhere
        Patience! Stay with me!
                            Judith Starr

The mother of Bevery Sills, the famous opera star, had an intense passion for music, especially for the opera. All day long she played records. By the time she was seven, Beverly had memorized the twenty-two arias from a collection of old Galli-Curci records—old seventy-eights—that she had heard daily throughout those early childhood years.

The Self-Image

"An individual's self-concept is the core of his personality. It affects every aspect of human behavior: ability to learn, capacity to grow and change, choice of friends, mates and careers. It's no exaggeration to say that a positive self-image is the best possible preparation for success in life," says Dr. Joyce Brothers, well-known psychologist and author.

"I know of no single factor that more greatly affects our ability to learn and perform well than the image we have of ourselves," writes Timothy Gallwey in his superb book, "Inner Tennis".

Since every parent wants to raise his child in the way that will provide her with this positive self-image, it's important that we know what actions and interplay with our children will lead to this growth. Although love is essential to the development of psychological health, Bruno Bettelheim, the well-known psychologist says, "Love is not enough." We must understand how the needs and the best interests of our children can be satisfied. It isn't enough to have "common sense", it isn't enough to rely on our own childhood experiences. Do you remember some of the things your parents did to you during your childhood or teen years that were so distasteful to you? And do you remember how you vowed that you would never do anything like that to your children? Then you found yourself acting in those same ways that had been repugnant to you. Learned responses take conscious effort to erase.

We have come to realize in our own parenting that we didn't always "know best", that some of our common sense didn't prove sufficient, that trying to learn and grow more lovingly sensitive to the needs and best interests of our children was the only way to becoming more effective parents.

Not all children are able to verbalize their needs, but our youngest son, David, was articulate and to the point. (Perhaps being the youngest child in a large family provided the necessary motivation!) From the time that his vocabulary allowed him to express his feelings he would come to us and get our immediate attention with one simple phrase — "I want you!" No interpretation or speculation was necessary on our part to know David's needs. We were most thankful for his help.

Yes, I Can!

If a child feels that she has an open-ended potential, that anything is possible, that the deciding factor is her desire, application and persistence, then life is a great adventure, not a threatening unknown.

Unfortunately, the words "I can't" are a staple in many people's thinking. The word "can't" is very potent. In itself it is just a symbol, but if you believe it and give it substance, it becomes reality, a very powerful force that stops the user dead in her tracks. The only antidote is "Yes, I can!" used daily and often. This becomes like an "Open Sesame!" . . . unleashing and unshackling mind and body.

If children approach a learning task with the handicap of a poor self-image, feeling defeated before they start, it's as though they're trying to run a race while dragging a ball and chain. To accomplish growth we have to be able to believe that we *can* grow!

One summer I was teaching at a Suzuki institute and had three thirteen-year-old girls in a small class. When I found that all three were in need of work on their vibratos, I decided to spend all of the class time on vibrato development. We tried many different approaches to vibrato, exercises that I demonstrated, then asked each girl to try in turn. They watched each other and me closely. I felt we were really getting somewhere as they started to improve slowly. On the third day, I received quite a shock. I was playing, passing closely in front of each girl while demonstrating a 'finished' vibrato that was perhaps too removed from the exercises we had been doing. "In the future you'll be able to vibrate this way," I said. "Do you think you'll be able to do just as well as I'm doing?" "Nope," said the first. The second replied, "I don't think so." Noting my incredulous look, the third girl backed off from a flat "No" by merely shrugging her shoulders.

"But how can you get a better vibrato if you don't believe you can do it?" I exclaimed. Grabbing my violin in my right hand, I tried to demonstrate a vibrato with that untrained hand. Of course, I couldn't do it. My vibrations were as stiff and jerky as theirs. "See! My right hands looks like yours. I'm not able to vibrate with it because I wasn't born with a natural ability to vibrate with either hand. I can vibrate easily with my left hand only because I developed that ability with persistent practice.

"I'm absolutely convinced that you three girls can all do as well. Of course, it won't work if you are convinced that you CAN'T! No matter what your teacher does to teach you, you will never have a beautiful vibrato *if you don't believe you can!"*

Parental-Family Responsibility

"Self-concept — who we are — we learn mostly from our family. This is why the family has an enormous responsibility. The most important thing in the world is that you make yourself the greatest, grandest, most wonderful, loving person in the world because this is what you are going to be giving to your children." This is what Leo Buscaglia has to say in "Living, Loving & Learning" about the family's influence on the self-concept of the child.

Stanley Coopersmith, associate professor of psychology at the University of California, studied 1738 normal middle-class boys and their families. The study began in the pre-adolescent period and followed through to manhood. He compared homes and childhood influences of the boys who had the highest self esteem with those of the boys having a much lower sense of self-worth. Three important characteristics were evident.

1. *High esteem children were clearly more loved and appreciated at home. Parental love was deep and genuine. The children were the object of the parents' pride and interest.*
2. *High esteem children had homes which fostered a more strict approach to discipline. During the latter part of the study it was found that the most successful, independent young men had come from homes that demanded strictest accountability and responsibility. Permissiveness in homes of lower esteem children created insecurity and dependence. Having no rules made children more likely to feel that no one cared enough to get involved.*
3. *High esteem children had homes characterized by democracy and openness. When boundaries for behavior were established there was*

freedom for individual personalities to grow and develop. They could express themselves without fear of ridicule. There was an overall atmosphere marked by acceptance and emotional safety.

Developing Attitudes of Self-Respect and Adequacy

"Parents seldom recognize how significant their verbal interactions with children are," say Dr. Don Dinkmeyer and Gary McKay in "Raising a Responsible Child." "The parent has considerable capacity and countless opportunities to build the child's feelings of self-respect and adequacy by indicating his pleasure in any accomplishment or effort the child makes." If a child faces a particularly difficult task, the best preparation the parent can give is to leave her with the attitude that the parent believes "You can do it". Then even if the child is not completely successful, the parent should make sure that the child knows that she has not slipped in the parents' estimation.

Even if parents attend athletic events, contests, or recitals where the child isn't completely successful, a supportive attitude should be shown:

I was really pleased to be there and to be your parent.

I am so glad that you played.

Even though everything didn't come off as you had hoped, I think it was a very good effort.

I can see that you made a lot of progress since last time.

I'm really proud of your hard work and good attitude.

Since feelings about self-worth are more difficult to change than physical performance scores, Suzuki's programming is very gradual so that small successes are planned. "Children like what they can do", Suzuki with his great insight often repeats. They like what they can do, as we all do, because of the wonderful feelings of self-worth that accompany an accomplishment, no matter how small.

What Did I Say!?!

With the child standing beside them, parents often discuss her weaknesses and shortcomings as though she were deaf, dumb, and blind. She doesn't seem to be listening, but maybe the child is smart enough to pretend *not to listen so that she can avoid embarrassment, or maybe she blocks out the words to avoid being hurt.*

In a class of four beginners, Janet, age 4, was progressing at a slower pace then the others. The children came at the same hour. Of course each had his individual lesson. This provided the environment for motivation that Suzuki suggests.

As the class was preparing to leave, Janet's mother stopped to talk to me. "Janet is very slow in catching on to new things. Her brother is so quick in everything he does, but Janet just seems to take a long time before she understands." Janet was standing at her elbow.

I wanted to protest. "Do you really think that Janet doesn't hear what you're saying? Do you realize that right now the word "slow" is probably being added to her inner descriptive file?"

Instead I tried to counter her negative remarks with positive ones. "Janet is a very attentive little girl. I like the way she listens and watches when I play for her. She always waits until I give her the signal to begin. Her bow and her posture at the keyboard are very good. I'm very happy to have her as a student."

Psychologists have observed that children do hear what is being said about them and most often will latch on to the key word or words and store them away for future use. What's the key word in the above conversation? Right - "slow". From that moment on (it's possible and probable that Janet has heard this before, of course) she has another piece to put in her image picture . . . "I am slow".

In "Your Child is Dying to Learn", Richard Gariepy says, "A vital fact with which parents must be acquainted is that your child is going to evaluate himself: he wants to know about himself and will come to some conclusion. He can only rely on what other people say and do, and on his interpretation of it."

Interpretations Vary

It is true that each unique human being will react differently to the same input, so we can't always be sure that what we say will have a negative result. This is where interpretation comes in. To some, a critical or negative evaluation will be a challenge to work and show what they can do. To others, it will be the trigger to give up, to rationalize failure.

An interesting story is told of twins who had an alcoholic father. Psychologists traced their paths in later life to see how their individual lives had progressed. One of the young men was an alcoholic like his father, the other a teetotaler. The remarkable thing was that when each was questioned as to the reason for his choice of life style, irrespective of the other each gave the same answer, "What would you expect with a father like mine?"

In spite of the unpredictable effect that our words might have, we must be always aware that casual, evaluative remarks about a child's qualifications are helping her to form her picture of herself. "He's good in English but doesn't have an aptitude for math". . . "She's just plain sloppy and always will be ". . . "She's so forgetful she'd leave her head behind if it weren't attached to her". . . "Betsy isn't good at any sport". . . "John will never learn to be responsible". Often we wonder why these comments and predictions become reality. Considering that this is the material we give the child to build the human being she is to become, it shouldn't be hard to understand.

Maybe all of us ought to remind ourselves everyday of something we often tell our children — "If you can't say something good, don't say anything!"

Erasing the Negative Self-Image

If a child states that she is stupid, ugly, or bad, there is nothing that we can say or do that will change that evaluation immediately. "A person's ingrained opinion of himself resists direct attempts at alteration," writes Dr. Haim Ginott in "Between Parent and Child". "As one child said to his father, 'I know you mean well, Dad, but I'm not that stupid to take your word that I'm bright!' If a child expresses a negative view of himself, our denials and protests only bring forth a stronger declaration of his convictions." Our best bet then is to show him that we understand the feelings that cause him to believe these things about himself.

Betty: I'm so dumb. I can't learn pieces as fast as Ann.

145

> Parent: You really think that you're not smart? You really feel that way?
>
> Betty: You said it!
>
> Parent: That makes you hurt inside, doesn't it?
>
> Betty: Yes. A lot.
>
> Parent: If you feel that way you're probably scared when you go to your lesson. You feel that your teacher will be disappointed that you haven't done enough, so you can't even play the part you've learned. Solo programs are probably embarrassing because the other kids you started with are playing pieces beyond yours. Well, Betty, I think you're a fine, capable person and I'm proud of you. It isn't how fast you learn, it's how well you play, and I'm proud of you and your work. Your opinion is quite different, but it doesn't change my opinion or my belief in you.

If parents have established a loving relationship with their children over a period of time, this kind of dialogue should sow some questioning doubts in the child's mind about her own conclusions.

Sometimes negative meaning may be given to what was meant to be a positive praising comment. A neighboring family had experienced the birth of an abnormal baby and had lived through the agony and pain of seeing a frail, sickly child deteriorate until she died at the age of two and a half years. Their next child, born three years later, was a lovely baby — a healthy and robust little girl with a beautifully formed body. One evening as the father was bathing the two year old child, he looked at her strong, sound body and remembering past experience, commented with admiration, "What a sturdy little girl you are!" Years later, as a teenager that girl told her parents, "You know, I have never felt very feminine or graceful. I've always thought of myself as the "sturdy" girl that Daddy told me I was when I was small."

Praise and the Self-Image

"You do not spoil your child or make him conceited by giving him genuine admiration and adulation", says Dr. Richard Robertiello in his book, "Hold Them Very Close, Then Let Them Go." "As a matter of fact the more of this you feel for him and express to him, the better self-image he will acquire."

Although we all recognize the human need of approval and praise, the way we frame our words of praise is of utmost importance to a child if she is to draw a realistic conclusion about her personality. Dr. Haim Ginott in "Between Parent and Child" says we should provide the child with "words like a magic canvas on which the child can't help but paint a positive picture of himself."

It is possible to give compliments that are ego-debasing instead of ego-building. "You are such an angel!" "What a wonderful boy!" These are the kinds of comments that make children squirm because they are wise enough to sense that they are being "buttered up" and insulted to think that the adult considers them stupid enough to be taken in. The child believes that the adult can't think of anything *really* good to say.

Instead, compliments that are specifically related to an accomplishment or effort are ways of giving the child realistic recognition of her abilities.

As an example, Bill, age 9 years, had volunteered to clean up the basement. He stacked up scattered boxes, rearranged and hung up tools on the peg board, threw away accumulated trash and swept the entire floor. When his mother came home she was obviously delighted.

"That basement was so messy I didn't think it could be cleaned up without a weeks work. There was so much trash and so many scattered boxes and tools that I thought it would be a mighty big job."

Bill replied, "I did it in 4 hours."

"It's so clean now, I think I'll come down here once a day just to enjoy looking at it! You did a fine thorough cleaning."

"I really like the way it looks", Bill beamed.

"So do I. Thank you very much, son," Mom said as she put her arm around his shoulder.

"You're welcome, Mom. It was kinda fun."

Can you imagine Bill's sense of pride in a job well done? He probably can't wait until his father comes home so that he can share his accomplishment and once again receive genuine appreciation and praise.

THE SELF-IMAGE

Music and Praise

Praise given a child who is studying music can also fall into the same desirable and undesirable categories. If we dwell on exaggerated generalized evaluations this can be embarrassing and uncomfortable. "You are the best musician I've ever heard." "Nobody's fingers can fly as fast as yours!" "I don't think anyone can play that better." Instead, the praise that focuses on accomplishment or effort is believable and acceptable. "That was very good practice this morning. You were attentive and careful." "That sixteenth note passage is very clear and rhythmical since you've worked on it." "You've learned an entire page today! Congratulations!" "What a beautiful tone you have in that melody!"

In response to our words of appreciation and praise for her efforts, the child draws positive conclusions about herself which she makes a permanent part of her self-image. These conclusions repeated internally by the child greatly determine her good opinion of herself and her world.

To sum it up, we need to remember that effective praise does not generalize. It recognizes specific good efforts, comments on and expresses gratitude for jobs well done, values achievements and creative ability. By its very nature it encourages and motivates the recipient.

Unconditional Love!

In a TV interview some time ago, John McKay, a great football coach at the University of Southern California was asked about his son's athletic talent. John, Jr. was a successful player on his dad's team. Coach McKay was asked to comment on the pride he must feel at his son's accomplishments on the field.

"Yes, I'm pleased that John had a good season last year. He does a fine job and I *am* proud of him. But I would be just as proud if he had never played the game at all."

Coach McKay is telling John that his human worth does not depend upon his ability to play football. If the next season brings failure and disappointment, John will not lose the respect of his father. His father's love is not dependent upon his performance. It would be nice if all parents could transmit this feeling to their children.

"The foundation of a solid relationship with our child is unconditional love," writes Dr. Ross Campbell in his book, "How to Really Love Your Child." "Only that type of love relationship can assure a child's growth to his full and total potential. If I only love my children when they meet my requirements or expectations, they will feel incompetent. They will believe it fruitless to do their best because it is never enough. Insecurity, anxiety, and low self-esteem will plague them and will be constant hindrances in their emotional and behavioral growth."

Campbell is quick to point out that no parent can successfully achieve this ideal one hundred percent of the time, but that shouldn't prevent us from being aware of its importance and constantly work toward that ideal.

As a parent and teacher, I have become increasingly aware of the consequences of conditional love. Our youngest child, David, has an exuberant personality and enthusiasm in abundance which is often a hindrance to serious focused attention. After a particularly trying practice time at the piano, I found myself withholding my love and attention to show my disapproval. "Mom, will you rub my back tonight?" David called from his bed later in the evening. "No, I'm too tired", I answered coldly. I was tempted not to answer at all! And guess what I found? . . . that David learned to use those same tactics on me in return! When I refused a request of his, he would withold his love from me . . . resist my hugs, avert my eye contact, or just fail to answer me. I had to face the fact that he learned well what I had taught him!

A few years ago I had an application for lessons from parents of a four year old girl and made arrangements for a meeting with them after a program. When the door opened, I saw, with some dismay, a sad looking mother with drooping eyes that 'cried', a down-turned mouth and a general look that said "Woe is me." The father behind her projected an unapproachable air of importance, stiff postured and humorless. "Jenny has been tested and found to be of genius capability", he pontificated. (Years ago when we were taking applications for a new Montessori class, I was astounded at the mumber of calls that started with "My Sara or my Tommy is far above average intelligence for his/her age." I always wondered where the 'average' children were with whom they were being compared!) And then I met Jenny, a darling little girl who realized how much her "smartness" meant to her parents. She had already learned to play games. When ever we came to something that she couldn't execute instantly, she pulled out her protective device . . . an attitude that said "I couldn't care less about this so why should I bother? It's not important to me." She felt that her parents' love depended upon her ability to be tops in all her efforts. Would anyone want to jeopardize that position? If she could feel that they loved her because she existed, because she was their daughter, because she was invaluable as a human being created by God, she would be able to chance it. She would be free to try and fail because she could always come back to loving arms.

Responsibility

The confidence and worthwhile feelings that accompany the child's acceptance of responsibility are worth the parental efforts. Actually children begin to enjoy being responsible. After all, it's very pleasant to be more independent, to learn new social skills, and to gain adult approval.

Here are a few suggestions for helping your child in his growth.

1. The child should be allowed to perform tasks that he can do for himself. Even though the results do not match adult standards, remember the product is not as important as the effort.
2. Training time must be relaxed. No time limits should be felt. Be sure you have enough time to allow him to work at his own pace.
3. Make a request, not a demand. Remember how you feel when someone tells you what to do instead of asking you. Children should be treated with the same consideration that adult relationships require.
4. Let natural and logical consequences occur. If the child refuses to perform a task that is his responsibility, and his alone, he must be allowed to experience the consequences. It is the parents' duty to stop talking, withdraw from conflict, and wait.

He deserves Paradise
Who makes his companions laugh.
                    The Koran

The only worry for parents should be to bring up their children as noble human beings. That is sufficient. If this is not their greatest hope, in the end the child may take a road contrary to their expectations. Your child plays very well. We must try to make him splendid in mind and heart also.
                    Shinichi Suzuki

Home Environment for Growth

Of all the gifts we can give our children the most far-reaching one is the positive environment we provide daily in our homes. Parents who show great love for music or exhibit great excitement and enthusiasm for any activity often find their children caught up by that emotional eagerness into the same pursuits. Suzuki's idea, right? The child is motivated by the obvious enjoyment of those around him.

In "A Touch of Wonder", a beautiful little book by Arthur Gordon, he says, "The easiest door to open for a child, usually, is one that leads to something you love yourself. All teachers (parents) know this. And all good teachers (parents) know the ultimate reward: the marvelous moment when the spark you are breathing on bursts into a flame that henceforth will burn brightly on its own."

If your children can feel and hear, both verbally and non-verbally, that you are excited by the possibilities for new growth and new opportunities in your own lives, they will catch your feelings and will be ready to embrace whatever challenges come into theirs. You are really living if each new day is begun with an anticipation that questions, "What new exciting things are in store for me today? I can't wait to find out! In some things I'll suceed, in others, I might fail, but they will be learning and growing experiences, no matter what the outcome."

Again Arthur Gordon says, "The real purpose, then, of trying to open doors for children is not to divert them or amuse ourselves; it is to build eager, outgoing attitudes toward the demanding and complicated business of living. This surely, is the most valuable legacy we can pass on to the next generation."

Encouragement Versus Pushing

I have often suggested to parents that they learn a new skill, preferably to play a musical instrument, during the time that their child is learning also. Have you ever heard that famous Indian quote, "Do not criticize another man until you have walked a mile in his moccasins"? Walking even a half mile in your child's moccasins can be helpful.

Our three daughters had learned to play recorders and enjoyed playing together. After Kathleen and Teresa had left home, Judith encouraged me to learn so she could have someone to play duets with her. I decided that I could spare fifteen minutes a day to practice, which made my progress a bit slow!

Judith walked in the kitchen holding her recorder two weeks after I'd started. "I've heard you practicing and you sound pretty good. Will you play a few of those simple duets with me . . . you know, the ones at the beginning of the book?"

"I'll try, but you'll have to be patient and be satisfied to do only those simple ones. I don't feel secure beyond the first ten pages."

We set up the stand in the music room and started on page one. After finishing page five, I was realy enjoying my accomplishment. "This is fun! Thanks for encouraging me to play."

"I knew you'd like it, Mom. Do you think we could try that last one a little faster?"

"I really don't think I can. That was just about my limit."

"You can do it, Mom, I know you can. Let's just try it anyway. I'll bet you'll do it easily."

We tried — and I didn't do it easily. The increased speed was just enough to confuse me because my responses had not yet become automatic.

"C'mon, Mom, let's try it once more. I'm sure you can do it," Judith repeated.

I stamped my foot. "No, I can't — not yet. Give me time to absorb what I've learned." Then I laughed and shook my head. "Just think how many times I've done this to you children, not accepting your own wise evaluation of where you were — always pushing for a little more."

The moral of the story is — if you want to be a more understanding, supportive parent to your child who is studying music, engage in the same activity yourself. You'll be more respectful of his feelings.

Expressions of Love — Eye Contact, Physical Contact

We can never find too many ways to express our love for our children. A child who is secure in the love of his parents, who knows beyond a doubt that this love is always there, is free to live fully.

"Eye contact—looking directly into the eyes of the child—and physical contact are both pleasant ways of giving a child the love that he so desperately needs," says Dr. Ross Campbell in "How To Really Love Your Child." If these ways of showing love are incorporated into our daily encounters with our children we will be able to meet their emotional needs.

Eye contact is often used by parents only when a child has accomplished some task that makes the parent proud. More often, eye contact is reserved for criticism or disapproval. If this is done habitually, although a young child may respond with obedience and docility, as he grows older resentment and anger will become the response. Making a habit of eye contact when your child talks to you or needs a reassuring glance is a worthwhile effort.

Naturally, the type of physical contact will vary with the age of the child. A young child, boy or girl, loves to be cuddled, kissed and hugged. Later, at seven or eight, children may want more rugged physical contact, wrestling, bear hugs, playful hitting. If the family has always engaged in a lot of physical affection throughout the early years, even adolescents do not reject those overtures which they have come to accept as natural expressions of those who care.

Our children, both boys and girls, were always demanding that Daddy play "sleeping dragon", a game he'd concocted during their early years. Daddy would lie down on the floor pretending to be asleep while they would courageously venture toward him, very, very quietly, sometimes daring to touch him, all the while knowing that at any moment he might suddenly grab them, growling and holding them in his grasp as they struggled to escape! Often he would have two or three of them in his power and then they would try to help one another to get free. This was a rather strenuous game for the "sleeping dragon". Even though at times it seemed to get a bit violent and I was tempted to stop it, I never did, and now I'm glad! It was a delightful way for them to fill their 'emotional tank' as Dr. Campbell puts it.

It is natural, too, for the Suzuki teacher and parent, to have eye contact and physical contact with the child who is taking a lesson or practicing. We, as teachers, are physically close to the young child when we teach individual lessons. As we direct and encourage them we maintain eye contact. It is the same with the parent during practice. Students will have their fingers placed correctly, their posture adjusted, their bow hold shaped, arm and hand movements patterned by the teacher or parent. Piano teachers and parents have the added opportunity of extra physical contact with beginners when they sit on the child's right, encircling the child with their left arm as they play the accompanying bass part to the melody. Most of the time children will welcome that kind of closeness and relax in the enclosed arm. Some students, though, will try to free themselves from the teacher's grasp as she prepares their hand for playing. This, perhaps, should be an obvious sign to the parent that the child should experience more physical affection at home. It does not mean that he doesn't want it . . . only that it has not been a part of his environment and he is unaccustomed to it. This awareness may be helpful to the entire family.

By caring for the child's emotional needs we are building security and confidence. Then the child is free to learn, to accept any learning experience as a welcome challenge. He is free to become the best that is in him.

A Sense of Humor!

The parent with that quick smile and sense of humor knows that most every situation can be dealt with more easily and more effectively when it can be viewed with a less than life-or-death manner.

In our partnership, I have always been the one with the too serious outlook. Bill has a way of sticking his chin out and assuming a kind of crackly voice and dialect that has forced many determined sad sacks in our family—including me—to laugh when we didn't want to! There's nothing more disgusting than finding yourself laughing when you really wanted to hold your austere, steely demeanor to impress people with the gravity of the situation! Now that I am alone with him and David, I haven't a chance to keep a straight face under any circumstances! (In spite of my complaints, I've been grateful over the years for that ever present sense of humor!)

A sense of humor is good for your health, too. Anger and its companion emotions are detrimental physically as well as emotionally. So keep smiling!

The Single Parent

There is no doubt that there are too many demands on the single parent who does not have the support system inherent in a partnership. The single parent who has a job allowing him to be home when he is needed is most fortunate. It is such an important priority that if at all possible, careerwise and financially, it should be a prerequisite for a choice of job. The part-time or seasonal job, of course, can fill this need perfectly.

Your parenting role should be the basis of your planning and decision. "How can I have enough quality time with my children? How can I be sure that by my scheduling I will transmit to them that they are a most important part of my life? How can I arrange to 'be there' when they need me for physical or emotional reasons?"

One busy single mother was always consulting her calendar when her children questioned her, "Mom, can we go shopping on Saturday afternoon?" "Will you take us to the show Friday night?" Her answer was, "Sorry, I have a previous engagement" or "No, I'm scheduled for an important meeting that evening." One day after a similar dialogue, her son replied, "Mom, aren't we important enough to be on your calendar, too?"

Even if you can't spend a couple of hours a day practicing with your child, if you consider the musical education of your child important, your involvement in Suzuki training can be a great respite and delight for both of you.

The Working Mother

There are now seventeen million women with children—more than half of all mothers in our country—who are working. We can say with assurance that the working mother is a permanent part of our social structure. Whether the decision to work has been made because of financial need or because of emotional need really doesn't matter.

In the past in our society, the child had the almost constant attention of the mother and father during his infancy, almost to the exclusion of anyone else. In this age of working mothers and busy fathers this is no longer true. When we realize that the early relationships are of such vital importance in the child's initial understanding of himself, we parents must take very seriously the choice of people and places that he will be exposed to in child care situations. The attitudes and reactions of parents and child care professionals are absorbed by the child and put into his computer for use later in his total evaluation of himself.

Recently I came across a book that I feel could be truly beneficial for all woman cast in this dual role. Called "Working Mothers" by Kay Kuzma, a working mother herself, it is filled with suggestions of all kinds for using time wisely and making sure that the quality of parenting will not be sacrificed. It addresses the most pressing problems— "Making the Most of Your Time Together, The Problems of Never Enough Time, Solving Job and Family Conflicts, Guilt, Illness and Fatigue, Meeting Personal and Family Needs" and many more.

I actually feel that there are working mothers who do a better job of mothering than some of their stay-at-home counterparts. A mother can remain at home and yet not give her children enough time or attention while the working mother tends to feel the need to plan more wisely to allow special areas of time specifically for her mothering job. So as with all problem situations, it's not the existence of the problem that matters it's how we see it and solve it that counts.

Actually your child's Suzuki involvement can fulfill some of that quality time. You can make the lessons and practice an oasis of enjoyment in the midst of inevitable bustling activity. Remember, music soothes the savage beast, so let it relax you and your child with the same soothing but valuable rewards!

TV or Not TV

Although there are families who have refused to let the TV set move into their homes and their lives, most families have accepted its presence for better or worse. Controversy continues to rage as to its value, its detrimental effect on the physical and emotional lives of our children, and its general long-range effect on our society.

My own personal feeling is similar to my feelings on good nutrition. It's not only an issue of right or wrong, good or bad. It's mostly that filling your stomach or your mind with something of little value means there is no room for more worthwhile or nutritious substances.

Not many people would invite undesirable characters to come in their front door and spend hours in their living room as guests. Neither should they be allowed to enter your living room or family room via the TV screen. We believe that parents should take an active part in planning and controlling TV viewing in the family. We have a duty to shield our children from a diet of sex and violence presented as acceptable ingredients of living.

When the hours of TV viewing are over what has been gained that is of lasting value? Those same hours spent learning a skill, exercising the imagination by reading or engaging in creative crafts and active sports, builds capability and strength of minds and bodies.

What are the physical liabilites of too much TV? For one thing, a lack of physical exercise. A report in Time magazine called "Those Tired Children" (Nov. '64) told of pediatricians at two Air Force Bases who were puzzled by a large group of children, ages 3 to 12, complaining of headaches, loss of sleep, chronic fatigue upset stomachs and vomiting. All of them were found to be TV addicts, watching three to six hours on weekdays, six to nine hours on weekends. When TV was forbidden and the rule was observed the symptoms disappeared. Those who did not obey the rule retained the symptoms.

TV is a great baby-sitter, if your requirements are just keeping the children occupied and out of your hair. But there is a price to pay. Our children are being fed a menu of Madison Ave. cleverness that builds desire for anything and everything that the market can produce to make dollars for its creators. This advertising is mixed with raw violence and murder that's dished up hour after hour with no redeeming features—neither originality nor artistic value.

TV has its place. There are some excellent educational and entertaining programs. Yet if it runs your home and your life, you'd better take a second look at your priorities. At one time we allowed no TV at all on school nights and a maximum of 2 or 3 hours on weekends if there was something of value. Now David watches "Leave It to Beaver" while he snacks after school. We feel this is a pleasant recreational interlude between the school day and resumption of homework or practice.

I've never been able to accept a Saturday morning filled with cartoon watching. Watching a cartoon is OK but hours and hours of it?! I don't think that should be a sacred commitment. So many times I have heard parents complain because of Saturday morning group scheduling . . . "But they'll miss cartoons!" I would think they would be glad for a substitute activity.

In the past we were told to guide our childrens' reading to the tales of great men and women in history, in every field, so that they would have instilled in them the fine qualities of character present in those great people. This is comparable to Suzuki's desire to have children hear and play the music of the great masters so that their hearts may become sensitive to great beauty and their lives may be enriched by such association. If we believe in this influence, how can we now expose our children to evil derelicts, insensitive criminals, and immoral lifestyles as though this will have no effect whatsoever on their thinking and their lives? It doesn't seem to make much sense.

Learning to play a musical instrument and practicing during those hours that might be passively spent sitting in front of the TV screen is a positive substitute, not just a time consuming activity. It's a good choice to make.

Please Treat Me Like a Perfect Stranger!

One evening as David and I were practicing following an afternoon of teaching, I realized that my voice was getting strained and tense. David turned to me, "Mom, how come you sound so different when you're working with your students then you do when you're working with me?" Out of the mouth of babes comes the reckoning with truth! Of course, I sounded different. I rarely become impatient or tense with my students, but often my own children didn't fare so well.

Turning it around, I once heard the story of the parent who, after enduring the grunt and run stage for some time, asked his teenager, "Please, just treat me like a perfect stranger."

Perhaps in many cases our own children would prefer to be treated as our neighbor's or friend's children. If we're honest we have to admit that they probably have a just criticism. Does familiarity have to breed irritation and impatience? Not really, if we are aware of the tendency to 'let down our hair' in family situations we can make the effort to eliminate it. It's worth a try.

To See Ourselves . . .

Suzuki advises mothers, "With your own child, please try to use the same expression, feeling, and language that you would use with others' children."

Our tone of voice, the words we use, and our facial expressions all reflect our inner attitude which to be the most effective, should be one of joy. Sometimes we try to disguise our real feelings rather than try to change our inner attitudes. Even when we use the correct words, our facial expressions may be disturbing to a child. And when we scold, our facial expression may become really frightening!

One Easter Sunday morning we had gathered the children outside for some home movies while they were dressed in their Easter finery. They kept running around enjoying the beauty of the morning and I was impatiently giving orders. "Get together so that I can take some pictures before you get those clothes dirty. Come on, Gregory, don't run over there! Kathy and Teresa, come back over to the porch. Now stay there for a minute." By the time I took the pictures the fake smiles were not very convincing!

"This camera is making a strange sound", I said irritably. Turning the camera around to see if the shutter was working properly, I pressed the trigger to start the camera. The shutter seemed to be working. I also noticed the red light was on indicating that there was no more film.

Two weeks later the film came back, and we settled down for an evening of the latest home movies. It was then that I found I was wrong about the last roll of film. There had been some film left even though the red light was on. Following the shots of the children, looking subdued but dutifully pleasant, a huge frightening face filled the screen! With one voice they yelled, "That's you Daddy! That's just how you looked!"

We rarely have the opportunity to see ourselves when we are scolding. Most of us wouldn't like what we saw. I know I didn't!

Traditions

Those of you who know "Fiddler on the Roof" have heard the great song, "Tradition". Although the rigidity of tradition is questioned in it, there is still a feeling of its value . . . of belonging, of meaning, of history.

Large families have a way of setting up traditions naturally. Our most extensive ones surround the Christmas season, beginning with the four week Advent season preceding Christmas. These have persisted through the years as a wonderful ribbon of continuity. When the older children come home bringing their spouses, they love to share these family activities with the new members. Even the things that they have admitted they disliked they still don't want to abolish—like having tomato soup and grilled cheese sandwiches for Christmas Eve supper! "Don't change it, Mom. We've always done it that way."

Tradition is important to the family sense of history—past and future. As children grow older, these constantly renewed memories give them a feeling of the importance of that history.

None of the events have to be elaborate or time taking—just a way of doing something that is "our family's" special way. You can incorporate musical activities into your festivities—a special piece of music, a special song, a home concert, or even bringing together a larger group to play together. You can be sure that your children will value those efforts even after they have established their own traditions for their own families.

Sharing Hospitality

We like to instill in our music students the feeling that they are giving a unique gift to others when they perform music. There are ways that families, too, can share their unique love and community with others outside that is good for children to experience.

During our older childrens' early years we were able to share our hospitality with many of the foreign students at our university. It

161

actually started because of our musical programs at international functions through which we were introduced to many of these students. Our children had many opportunities to meet and develop lasting friendships with people from Africa, Iraq, Malta, Costa Rica, Bolivia, England, Phillipines, Taiwan, and Venezuela. Many of these students liked music and were extremely appreciative of impromptu concerts at our home.

While our children felt that they made a vital contribution to the family hospitality, they knew that they were the recipients of much more. They gained understanding and knowledge of other peoples and cultures first hand. One of our dearly beloved friends, an Iraqi lawyer and political scientist, who returned to Baghdad because of family illness never returned to the U.S. He was shot in a political reprisal. We'll never forget him—he enriched our lives by his presence.

The Arabic students loved to hear Bill play the Monti "Czardas" and would clap, sing, and dance with great enthusiasm throughout the performance.

All of our guests haven't been foreign students, of course. For children to grow 'outward' they need to be encouraged to open their hearts and help their parents share the warmth of music and home.

Don't part with your illusions
When they are gone you may still exist
But you will have ceased to live.
                              Mark Twain

                    I will sing to the Lord all my life,
                    Make music to my God while I live.
                                        Psalm 103

In Vienna during the period that Franz Shubert was a child, it was not unusual for families to make music together in the evenings. The Shubert family sang the latest songs, played the latest waltzes, string quartets, and often joined with other families to do larger more serious works. By the time Franz was ten he had outgrown his violin teacher and was sent to the local choirmaster who taught him piano, organ, violin, singing, and music theory.

Family Lifestyles

It is often said in Japan that the 'only' child or the 'one-child' family has the best environment for success in Suzuki's Talent Education method. It is true that quite a few of the outstanding students in Japan were 'only' children. Of course, that statement didn't do much to encourage the Starr family, since there was no way to retrace our steps and qualify!

A family's lifestyle does have a significant bearing on the accomplishments of children. An only child who has no sibling interference or distraction, whose time at home is spent mostly in the company of adults, has quite a different environment from the child who has brothers and sisters, or even one brother or sister. The mother's and father's attention need not be divided. The mother with one child may have the opportunity, if she wishes, to spend all of her free time working or playing with this one child. If she does not have a job outside of the home, she should have adequate time for maintaining the home and family plus pursuing some interests of her own. This makes a more calm, relaxed mother and consequently, a more calm and relaxed family atmosphere.

Parent Priorities

If I had the opportunity to re-live my life, knowing what I do now, I would take a second look at my own personal commitments during the time that our children were small. During the years of my children's infancy and early childhood, I would have curtailed my outside activities. (I know that in my case that would have involved many years, but in a smaller family of two children who are close in age, that would be only a matter of a few years.) I don't mean that the mother should be cloistered at home every minute, but her top priority should be her mothering. My teaching, accompanying, playing in a string quartet and the local symphony took too much time away from my children . . . in my case not from my husband, of course, because most of the time we were working together professionally.

164

I remember one unforgettable experience when our second daughter, Teresa was three years old. I was preparing the Grieg Concerto for a performance with the Knoxville Symphony, so as the concert date neared I was practicing many hours a day. Teresa was a very outgoing, animated little girl who communicated her feelings openly. Naptime was over and Teresa came into the living room as I sat down at the piano. She threw herself on the floor beside me, kicked and screamed, "No prac'ice, Mommy, NO PRAC'ICE! NO PRAC'ICE!" I didn't need an interpreter to know her feelings. She felt cheated of my time and attention, and she felt it strongly!

Every privilege carries with it a responsibility. The privilege of having loving, happy, well-adjusted children makes time demands upon both mother and father. There are necessary sacrifices to make, as with all worthwhile goals and activities.

Evaluate your own feelings. Do you think you give your child enough of yourself? Or do you assuage your guilt feelings by giving your child everything else and letting others give him love and attention and keep him busy?

Perhaps most of all we need a change of attitude toward child rearing. Being a parent is perhaps the most important job in the world . . . building and nurturing the human person is certainly more important than building a bridge or a skyscraper or even writing a great piece of literature. We are helping to form the future creator of those buildings, the painter of those masterpieces, and the composer of those compositions. In that way we are helping to mold the future.

Children's Priorities

All parents want to give their children all the benefits that exist in abundance in our society. Yet we simply can't succumb to the fear that our children will not be "fulfilled" or "well-rounded" if they are not exposed to every available stimulation in the academic and social environment. Flitting from one activity to another and remaining mediocre in all destroys a good self-image and causes inner conflict. Children are robbed of the wonderful 'high' that comes from working hard, learning and accomplishing in depth in one field of activity. To do something well, while using all one's resources and abilities, builds true happiness and confidence. Then the person can say with conviction, "I like myself!"

When a child comes to a parent asking to participate in some sport or lessons, it would be a good time to explain to the child what his responsibility will be. Often the child is soon over the first flush of "something new" and the daily routine of work and sameness is not so desirable. If the parent has explained the child's obligations beforehand, it is easier to again remind him of those obligations. Perhaps in the future, because of his experience, the child as well as the parent will be able to weigh the time and effort that an added activity will require and make knowledgeable decisions that benefit *both* parent and child.

Evaluating your children's activities as to priorities is very important to their futures. First, you must know your child. What are his physical needs? Is he active, needing ample physical play and outdoor activity? What are the needs for sleep?. . .eating habits, etc. In other words does a heavy schedule interfere with getting to sleep or eating properly? Some children show obvious results of over extended activities. These are easy to observe, but the child who internalizes the stress is more difficult to see. It is a known fact that ulcers, a stress disease, as well as mental illness, have increased in the early childhood years. Dr. Ross Campbell, well-known psychiatrist, says that the age of children needing psychiatric help has plummeted to six and seven years of age where in the past it was mostly needed by pre-teens and teens. Too much pressure is a contributing factor to this alarming trend.

Physical Activity

A good balance of physical and mental activity is important. Suzuki has spoken so often of the importance of physical development that produces quick, facile movement. We parents of Suzuki students should be especially sensitive to this important facet of our child's growth and pick extracurricular activities that offer such opportunities. In making decisions on childrens' schedules, try to balance dancing, skating, gymnastics, or a team sport with musical pursuits.

The child who is well coordinated physically should excel in both areas.

Michael was four when he attended the Talent Education kindergarten in Japan. One diminuitive little girl, Reiko, appointed herself as Michael's guardian. Although Michael was a head taller than Reiko, she was his constant guide and companion. Numerous slides and snapshots show them standing together, hand in hand! But one thing bothered Michael . . . Reiko could jump rope, fast and without faltering, while the rope got tangled in Michael's feet after one hesitant jump. Our combination cook, interpreter and friend, Mikiko, found this disturbing also and decided to accompany him to school to survey the problem. She found that what Michael said was true. With Mikiko's help and much effort Michael improved.

Our next oldest son, Billy, Jr., attended first grade at Genshi Elementary School, about a block away from our house in Matsumoto. On his first report card there appeared a comment on his "clumsiness". It was obvious that this was considered important to his overall performance in school. Calisthenics were a daily activity, done each morning on the school playground to the strains of the Colonel Bogey March played over loud speakers. From our house we could hear it loud and clear! His last report card had this comment on it: "Billy has improved in physical activities. He is no longer clumsy."

Not only children, but Japanese adults consider physical activity important to overall performance. This summer (1983) while we were in Matsumoto for the International Conference, we looked down from our hotel window on a construction site below. It was early morning and work had not yet begun, but in the open area adjacent to the new building the workers were lined up in front of a gentleman who was leading them through vigorous calisthenics. Years before when we had lived in Matsumoto we had noticed that during lunch hour business employees played ball or exercised. What a much more stimulating way to prepare for a full day or an afternoon of work than to linger lethargically over a second cup of coffee or dessert!

Musical Activity

It has been said, and we firmly agree, that a regular practice time should be established, and the practicing should be done at that same time each day. But *in many families—ours included—that was an impossibility. If we tried to establish an after school time for our pianists, that could be done on only two days of the week because I taught on the others and the piano was not available. If an after dinner time seemed desirable we were reminded that swimming took place on two weeknights. Other irregularities kept popping up in parents' or childrens' schedules. A half hour in the morning for part of the practice was least in danger of being superseded . . . unless activities of the night before made the early rising time not feasible!*

Sound familiar? Even if you don't have as many children as we did, you are still able to identify with scheduling problems, I'm sure.

I can say that our year in Japan was much less hectic and so wonderful for me because of help with shopping and the cooking of meals. I was able to spend more time with the children and even practice some myself, which I hadn't done with any regularity for quite a few years. The cold winter evenings were spent together huddled near the kerosene stoves, reading, talking or writing letters. I even had time to knit scarves and mittens for everyone! I often said that my "culture shock" was greatest upon our return to the States!

In spite of the problems, priorities do have to be established within the framework of your own unique family's lifestyle. If you consider that music education is important in your child's life, some sacrifices have to be made by both parent and child. Parents must be prepared to give time and effort to support and guide the child's musical growth, an inherent part of Suzuki philosophy. The parent may need to terminate some personal pursuits to be available for practice time . . . but it needs to be done willingly and pleasantly, without the "I'm doing this all for you when I'd rather be doing something else" expression on the face and in body language. If you don't enjoy it, don't expect the child to enjoy it. He gets the message clearly.

Plan and Persevere

Some parents seem to feel that a child should have every spare minute filled. So poor Mary or Kevin goes to dancing on Monday, skating on Tuesday, drama on Wednesday, crafts on Thursday and music lesson on Friday. Personally, we believe there should be some unscheduled time, time left for 'doing nothing', 'day-dreaming'! The spirit as well as the mind and body needs the nourishment that comes from quiet moments.

Family lifestyles do differ. . . in myriads of ways. The important decisions must be made to complement and enrich each unique family unit. Do you really want to pursue the course of Suzuki training enough to reevaluate and adjust your time priorities where necessary, and help your child do the same? If you answer affirmatively, be firm and persistent in your pursuit, so that your child and you will have a rewarding and worthwhile experience. They will thank you in a few years, and you will thank God that you had the foresight to participate in such a life enriching opportunity!

Health and cheerfulness mutually beget each other.
Joseph Addison

There is no duty we so under-rate
As the duty of being happy.
Robert Louis Stevenson

Humanity is fortunate
Because no man is unhappy
Except by his own fault.
Seneca

Sibling Rivalry

The Grass is Greener

Mom and Dad had been vacationing for two weeks in Hawaii. On the day they were to leave for home they spent many hours exploring toy and gift shops searching for presents to take home to John and Jim, their six-year-old twin sons. The agonizing decision resulted in identical T shirts, white with a green surfer on green waves, "Hawaii" printed in green script letters across the top.

Mom and Dad were barely out of the car when both boys flew out of the front door to greet them. The boys took turns hugging each parent and after the luggage was carried in, they all sat down in the kitchen for a snack. "Oh, yes", Dad said as he suddenly pushed his chair away from the table, "before we listen to you tell us all about what you did while we were away, we have something we want to give you". When Dad returned he carried the two packages. "We thought you might like these". Both parents smiled expectantly as the boys ripped open the packages. There was a moment's hesitation - then John dropped his shirt and grabbed Jim's. "I want his!" he spouted with vehemence.

A Place in the Sun

It isn't too difficult to understand the basis of sibling rivalry. Each human being needs her own place "in the sun", and so every child needs to feel that she is getting a fair share of those loving sun's rays provided by her parents. "Am I really as important to them as Jim is?. . . Do they really love me as much as they love John?. . . Why did Daddy play two games with Jim and only one with me?"

Of course, the child who has brothers or sisters is confronted daily with having to share and be satisfied with a portion of her parents' time and attention. The only child may confront a similar situation if a parent or parents are involved with a career or hobby that swallows the time she feels rightfully belongs to her.

171

Plan Activities to Avoid Natural Conflict

Because of this very sensitive area in childrens' lives it is certainly best to plan activities that will not provide ground for such feelings. For that reason in the music study area there are a few simple guidelines to help you plan realistically to try to avoid the natural conflicts that may occur.

1. Children in the same family should be encouraged to study different instruments whenever possible.
2. If children in the same family do have the desire to play the same instrument and cannot be dissuaded, their starting times should be staggered, i.e. one child should begin a year or two before the other, or might study with a different teacher.
3. Parents (and teachers, too, of course) should avoid comparison. Statements such as "I wish you'd practice as much as . . . be as enthusiastic as . . . learn as fast as . . ." only provide fertile ground for resentment and hateful feelings toward the person to whom they are being compared. If it's a family member, that's disastrous.
4. If at all feasible, the choice of the instrument (which you have already narrowed down beforehand) should be discussed with the child. She should know that her thoughts and feelings are worth considering. At the same time, guidance as to the wisdom of her choice should be given.

Peace or Strife

Even the most conscientious parents who provide adequate time and attention for their children are often disturbed by the lack of peace in family life. "Perhaps the most important idea (for parents) is to give up any Utopian ideal that you may have of a household of children getting along nicely with each other without fighting," says the Gesell Institute's book on "Child Behavior". It is somewhat comforting to know that your children are not abnormal, or that you are not bad parents.

Since I was an only child who felt deprived because I had no brothers or sisters, Bill's tales of life in a family of six children sounded like heaven to me who had felt so alone in a world of adults. Of course, he never embellished the reminiscences with any of the realism of bickering, disagreements, or just plain fighting. I honestly don't think he remembered them as being a part of it. God is good in this way as in so many others. We seem to forget the unpleasant things that surround an otherwise pleasant occasion. So my version of idyllic family life was nurtured. Why should children fight at all? If the home were filled with love and caring, if they loved each other, why? I visualized our future home in a daily setting of peace with enthusiastic activity. It took years for Bill to convince me that anything else could be normal! Yet, it is one thing to recognize the inevitability of occasional bickering and fighting and another to try to do something about it so that daily family life may be more tranquil.

This Too Shall Pass

As we mentioned above in reference to music study, planning ahead with alternatives when we can see situations coming that would be sure to cause conflict is one way to avoid explosive situations. It's really worth the effort. And then there is a most comforting thought that has soothed my distraught mind often at times such as these . . . "This, too, shall pass". And it does. With children advancing in age the teasing, bickering, squabbling and wrestling all become a thing of the past.

Now that we have grown children who with their diverse personalities have provided us with experiences of all kinds, we can comfortingly offer consolation to other parents because we have seen and are experiencing that "calm after the storm". In our family, Teresa and Gregory, our second and third children, were like dynamite and match to each other . . . the role of dynamite and match alternating between them! The fact that they were only a year apart in age may have contributed to the problem. Today, as our oldest children have become young adults, we observe with joy the new dimensions of loving relationships that are evident in the family network. And it is our turn to forget the struggle of those earlier days . . . and when we do remember, to agree wholeheartedly that it was all worth it!

Write on your hearts
That everyday is the best day of the year.
                                                    Emerson

Even before they learned to read or write, Jerome Kern and his brother began to study the piano. His mother's love of music and her devotion to the piano inspired in her sons the love of good music. During later years Jerome remembered with nostalgia the little impromptu concerts which he, his mother and his brother often gave in the family living room.

Nutrition

Does It Matter What We Eat?

Today more and more people are thinking about the kind of food they eat and the effect that it has on their bodies and minds. They are realizing that it is illogical to carefully maintain a car with high quality gasoline and motor oil and not consider the quality of the food they eat to maintain the much more complex human being.

Sometimes we need personal experiences to make us aware of our nutritional needs. At the time when our three oldest children were five, three, and two, my own personal world seemed to be falling apart. I loved my family dearly. I had three beautiful, normal, healthy children and a thoughtful, loving husband who was supportive and encouraging. I couldn't understand why I felt so drained physically and mentally. I was exhausted much of the time. The mid-morning of each day would find me shaky and dizzy. Feeding lunch to the children was a tremendous effort. My only goal was to get them down for a nap, so that I could lie down to rest.

My activities, shopping and household chores were often done in a 'fog'. The voices of people talking to me sounded as though they were coming from a distant planet. Naturally, you can imagine that I began to wonder about my mental health. However, I rationalized that this was probably the natural state of affairs for a mother with small children who kept busy professionally.

Sometime later, Betty Newell, a dear caring friend and fellow symphony violist, presented me with a book by the famous pioneer nutritionist, Adele Davis. Tactfully she told me that she had noticed how tired we had been looking during symphony rehearsals, and she hoped this might help. Feeling as badly as I did, I started reading the book voraciously. Here I found that all of my symptoms pointed to hypoglycemia, or low blood sugar. I began to eliminate sugar and multiply protein intake in our diet. This was the turning point in the health of our family.

NUTRITION

Needless to say, I don't claim to be an expert in the field of nutrition, but I have been so happy with my own and our family's great improvement in mental and physical health that I've wanted to share our story with others. For years our medical expenses have been so low that we have been unable to qualify for any medical deductions on our income tax! That's not bad for a family of ten! It must mean that we're doing something right!

Food Affects Behavior

We are hearing with increasing frequency about hyperactivity, allergies, and the inability to concentrate. We have been told of the harmful effects of junk foods and sugar, and yet most children, and teenagers in particular, are downing gallons of carbonated sweet drinks. One pediatrician observed that the record among his patients was 98 gallons of cola in two months! Younger children are drinking more of the powdered sweet drinks and the 'fruit drinks' which many mothers use as inexpensive substitutes for real fruit juices. The labels on these drinks state "10% fruit juice" and the two top ingredients, listed in order of highest content, are water and sugar.

Dr. Derrick Lonsdale, who heads the biochemical genetics section at the Cleveland Clinic's Center for Children and Youth, says that some behavior accepted as typical of teenagers might be symptoms of what has popularly become known as the "junk food phenomenon". "I think it's going unrecognized. It's being treated as neurosis, nervousness, plain bullheadedness, or 'It's his personality, you know. He's growing up.' " Dr. Lonsdale believes that this approach to diet is changing the balance of neurological transmission which is the hallmark of the function of the brain and the central nervous system. "It means", emphasizes Dr. Lonsdale, "that the quality and quantity of nutrition can change your behavior. That's the bottom line!"

Sugar—A Danger Zone

Children and adults, too, have allowed themselves to be educated to a great extent by those who produce food for profit. Where do our children hear about the merits of the latest sugary cereals? From the

176

ads on TV that are aimed directly at them. And many parents, even though they actually know better, go ahead and buy the products because they can't stand the pressure! That is just what the big commercial interests are counting on.

Consumer Reports, March 1978, in the article "Too Much Sugar", points out that much of the food industry operates on the assumption that the consumer has three taste preferences - sweet, sweeter and sweetest. For that reason we find sugar in table salt, hot dogs, most cold meats, toothpaste, catsup, creamers, soft drinks, peanut butter, yogurt, salad dressings, and baby foods. In fact, I recently learned that if catsup is made without sugar the label must read "imitation catsup"! Sugar is everywhere, as we realize when we start reading labels on the food products we buy. Remember that the first ingredient on the label is the chief ingredient in the product, and the others are listed in the order of their prominence.

The late Senator Hubert Humphrey, before the Senate Select Committee on Nutrition in the U.S. Senate, stated, "Having undergone surgery recently for cancer, the more I read about this the more I could literally weep over my dietary habits over the years. The evidence is there on sugar. The evidence you present is unmistakeable scientific evidence, but how do you compete against an ad on television?"

In his book, "Feed Your Kids Right", Dr. Lendon Smith, a former Clinical Professor of Pediatrics at the University of Oregon Medical School and a member of the American Academy of Pediatrics says, "Some mothers are afraid to take a strong stand on sound family nutrition because they are afraid that their children will not love them if they don't provide sweet foods".

Research Proves Effects of Sugar

The research of numerous biochemists and physicians documents the harmful effects of excessive sugar ingestion. All conscious bodily activity is initiated in the cerebral cortex of the brain and in order to adequately function it needs a constant flow of glucose. An imbalance of blood sugar can cause the cortex to respond to stimuli with bizarre behavior. Complex foods which produce a gradual breakdown into

177

glucose provide the steady, even flow required by the cortex and the entire body. In contrast, when there is an intake of refined sugar, the pancreas responds with over-production of insulin to metabolize it and the blood sugar level falls suddenly and drastically. A sensitive person can become anti-social, depressed, or may have a variety of psychosomatic symptoms. This is called "the roller coaster" syndrome because the subject usually eats something sweet to make him feel better, and the whole sequence starts all over again! It is estimated that 50% of the American people are afflicted with this condition . . . a great number of children among them, of course.

A study published in March 1981 was done by two University of Michigan scientists on the total sugar intake of 657 randomly selected children, five to twelve years of age. The study found that these children were consuming on the average of 134 grams (about 1/4 pound) of sugar per day. Some of the children studied were using as much as 280 grams (1/2 pound) a day! This came mostly from sweetened beverages, cakes, cookies, pies and other desserts and fruit juices.

Learning and Diet

An article called "Why Johnny Can't Learn - A Surprising Answer" by Lawrence Galton, cited a study made at the New York Institute for Child Development. Of 265 hyperkinetic children (children who have an abnormal amount of uncontrollable muscular movement often resulting in inability to concentrate or learn) who were tested for glucose-tolerance, 74% showed abnormalities. In other words, high sugar and refined carbohydrate intake stimulated the insulin production that causes blood sugar to plummet and produce the behavior associated with hyperkinetic children. The Institute's multi-faceted treatment of these children included six high protein feedings a day, reduced intake of sweets and refined carbohydrates and as much as possible the elimination of artificial colors and flavors from their diet.

"I've taught in schools from ghetto to upperclass and seen the behavior dysfunction when children came in at 8 a.m. munching on a candy bar or doughnut and sipping a cola", says Mary Ann Pickard in the preface to her cookbook "Feasting Naturally". "And sending them off with a sugary breakfast cereal, white toast and jelly with a pre-sweetened Vit. C drink is no better! No wonder the discipline situation in our schools is such a nightmare!"

Sweet Holidays—Sour Aftermath

So many times teachers and parents are aware of the problems in concentration and personality that occur at the time of holidays, birthday parties, and similar breaks from routine. We often have chalked it up to excitement, but it is wise to try to understand why these deviations occur. If we do, we can try to do something about the kind of food the children consume during those holiday celebrations.

"Too many sweets can turn some usually agreeable children into monsters at home and in school. Many children simply cannot handle the over-large doses of sugar in Halloween candy, for instance. Too much sugar can cause irritability, disruptive behavior, decreased attention span and loss of concentration. Parents and teachers have told us they dread this post-Halloween period. There are arguments and fights at home, and classes the next day are virtually unmanageable, with children agitated and restless", says Dr. Jerome Vogel, medical director of the New York Institute for Child Development. This Institute for Child Development has dealt with more than 3,000 children with learning problems. They have found over the years since 1968, when their non-profit institute was founded, that nutrition can play a major role in many learning and behavioral problems.

Hidden Additives

In 1975 Dr. Ben Feingold, a California pediatrician and allergist, outlined a diet for children who were considered to have symptoms of hyperactivity. It has since received nationwide attention and the testimonies of parents who have been given hope and help after years of frustration testify to its effectiveness in a large percentage of cases. This diet forbids all foods that contain certain dyes and other additives as well as foods that are rich in salicylates. (Salicylates are a group of compounds related to salicylic acid in their basic structure and are present in a number of fruits, and vegetables, as well as beverages and medications.) Eighty-five percent of the food not permitted in this diet is in the category of high sugar. Chemical additives found to be so destructive to childrens' behavior are found in largest amounts in junk foods. And junk foods include the following: candy and candy bars, all cookies, all packaged desserts and beverages such as puddings, gelatins, instant drinks, all soft drinks, most "convenience" foods in packages (muffins, biscuits, cookies, cakes), all ice creams, except those which specify on the label that they do not contain any additives. All of these foods, if bought at the supermarket, are likely to be loaded with dyes, synthetic flavorings, preservatives, thickeners, surface active agents, sequestrants, stabilizers, starch modifiers, texturizers, binders, anti-caking agents and on and on and on. These are the hidden additives that can do so much damage.

What About Adults?

Children are not the only ones affected by additives and the consumption of sugar. Numerous adults have experimented with the elimination of these offending foods and found that their health improved significantly. If you suspect that you might benefit from such a regime why not try it? Things like frequent headaches, chronic fatigue, and a lack of general vitality are often attributable to diet. There's really nothing to lose except a bit of effort, and there could be a lot to gain!

After discussing this together, Bill and I decided to analyze our food intake to see if we were inadvertently getting more than we meant to have of these additives and sugar. First, we don't buy refined sugar, but instead use honey and fructose (fruit sugar) when we need sweeteners. We use honey at the table and honey and fructose in baking and occasional desserts. Sometimes critics equate honey and fructose with refined sugar, saying all sugar is alike. Naturally we should not ingest large amounts of any sugars. However, you will remember that earlier in this chapter we compared the body's reaction to complex foods which produce a gradual breakdown into glucose, allowing a steady even flow to the brain and body, to the body's reaction to refined sugar which needs no breaking down. With refined sugar the pancreas responds with an overproduction of insulin to metabolize it all at once, thereby causing the blood sugar to fall drastically immediately afterward because it has been instantaneously metabolized. Both honey and fructose are complex foods which produce the gradual breakdown.

Second, we buy no packaged foods, no sugar cereals, no soft drinks or Koolaid type drinks. Our shopping consists mostly of fresh fruits and vegetables, real fruit juices, whole grain breads, flours, and cereals, natural cheeses, and snack foods such as chips without preservatives that are purchased at health food stores. To the statement that these foods are more expensive, I would answer that if their volume would increase, the prices would go down. As it is, we would rather spend money on preventative measures for health than pay for medical treatment that will try to repair the damage caused by poor nutrition. This reminds me of a statement I heard recently about the value of exercise, "If you don't take time to exercise, you'll take time later for illness". I think the same could be said about diet. if you don't spend money on foods that build health, you will spend it later on medical care. Nature has a way of balancing the books and somehow she can never be fooled!

School Lunches—Nutrition in Action

In the Fulton County Schools of Atlanta, Georgia, Sara Sloan is a one woman dynamo who has completely revised the eating habits of the schools where she is Director of Food and Nutrition Programs. The program, in existence since 1976, is called "Nutra", the Natural Program. It features natural whole foods, low in fat and salt with no artificial coloring, additives, preservatives, or refined carbohydrates. She schedules workshops to educate teachers, parents, and children, has "mini" Nutrition Time in the classroom, and nutrition blurbs on the school intercom. Walking through the halls in her schools you would hear . . . "Try the "real thing" - See the pot of grass (sprouts) in the cafeteria. Interested in growing your own? Contact our cafeteria manager" or "Are you a Hot Fudge Sundae? You are what you eat. Is your behavior pattern like a hot fudge sundae - Smooth and creamy and sometimes bittersweet? Sugary snacks create mood swings and put you in an energy slump. Hardboiled eggs, fruit, seeds, nuts, cheese, yogurt, kefir, tofu give you more bounce per ounce for feeling fit energy".

And has her program been successful? The increased student participation in the school lunch program attests to that - an increase from 61% to 87%. This is the first school system in the nation with a program eliminating refined sugar in school meals for children. "The success of the Nutra Program has proven", Ms. Sloan says, "that when children are educated and involved in growing, preparing and cooking food, they will eat those foods even if the food is new and unfamiliar".

Courage to be Different

For quite a few years now our family has been "different" in our eating habits. At certain ages the children have suffered some ridicule for this, and we've tried to be sympathetic and supportive while educating them to the reasons behind our diet. Generally speaking, they have been cooperative and open minded, and it has been pleasing to see their spirit of acceptance.

When David, our youngest son, was in fourth grade, he had one particular lunchroom antagonist who eagerly waited each day as David opened his lunch box to see what "yuky, weird" thing would be exposed to his scrutiny. Of course, he was quick to call everybody's attention to "what David brought today"! One particular object of examination was a bag of green pepper sticks. For some reason nobody had ever eaten raw green pepper sticks before—they smelled and looked weird! Alfalfa sprouts on sandwiches were also a novelty, but David discovered a new tactic. He asked people if they wanted to taste them. One morning as I prepared his lunch, he came into the kitchen. "Mom", he said, "Can you put more sprouts in a sandwich bag? Lots of the kids are asking me for them, and I don't have enough for myself and them, too". My 'hallelujahs' had to remain silent.

One of our older sons, Bill, Jr., an architecture student who is spending this school year ('82-'83) studying at Waseda University in

Tokyo, Japan, lived in a dorm during his freshman year at Cornell. The following year he moved into a house with ten other students who divided household and cooking chores. Many of them were vegetarians and most of them were serious about a diet of natural and whole foods.

During the Christmas vacation in the middle of that year we were talking about what kind of meals they had prepared. "It's really strange", he said. "Most of the kids haven't had a lot of the food at home that they're cooking and eating now. I think they feel as though they've discovered something "different" by themselves—almost like a kind of rebellion. But when they ask me if I've tasted some of the things they make, I always say 'Sure, we have that at home'. They say they want to meet you, because you sound like such neat parents". Fortunately, Bill has not felt the need to rebel in any other way to make up for our not providing him with this harmless outlet!

So don't be afraid to help your children by educating and providing them with food that builds instead of destroys. If you can weather the storms and stick to your convictions in this as in other important areas, you will probably qualify in their book as "neat" parents!

The Tide Changes

All in all, we have been heartened over the years to see the changes in the eating habits of a large percentage of the people in our range of contact. Years ago receptions given after recitals at the University of Tennessee used to consist of the usual sweet punch, cakes and cookies. In the past few years, however, the Sigma Alpha Iota music sorority girls have been serving fruit juices, cheeses, raw vegetables and dip, and whole grain crackers and chips. These have been consumed with enthusiasm!

When Suzuki came to our campus in 1981, his visit attracted 800 youngsters and their parents from all over the Southeast. At this time the SAI music sorority under the direction of Mary Ann Goodwin, then a Suzuki teacher trainee, decided to fill a dual purpose by providing good wholesome food and drinks for the children while at the same time raising funds for their group. They didn't realize how popular their offerings would be. They were swamped! Within a short period of time their total inventory was sold out! Many of the parents came to thank them for their thoughtfulness. It was only after they closed down their booth that the soft drink vendors were able to do much business.

Nutritional Snacks

Suzuki teachers really appreciate working with children who are attentive and relaxed during their lessons. Many teachers have noticed improvement in the children's behavior at lessons after they have requested that parents try to provide good nutritious snacks before lesson time. Here is a helpful list you might wish to consult.

Acceptable snacks: Fruit or real fruit drinks, milk, popcorn, nuts, cheeses, peanut butter, whole grain crackers or chips without additives.

Taboo snacks: Cokes and all soft drinks that contain caffeine, sugared drink mixes, ice cream, candy or candy bars, cookies, cake.

With a little planning the elimination of sugary and additive filled foods can be accomplished. Try it—you'll like it!—and you'll especially like what it does for your children.

Parents' Nutritional Needs

Adults, as well as children, have nutritional needs which, if not satisfied, can lead to inability to cope with the physical and emotional stresses of parenthood - or of any other occupation for that matter. Parents cannot say "Do as I say, not as I do" and consider it good advice. A recent television spot shows a mother eating "junk food" as she sadly delivers a lecture. "Kids just don't eat right. You tell them what's good for them, but they just won't listen!" she says as she munches away.

"Your ability to handle anger is influenced by many things, most of which have nothing to do with the actions of your teenager", says Dr. Ross Campbell in his book "How to Really Love Your Teenager." "One of these is your physical condition. Are you eating foods that will help you feel your best? Most authorities consider breakfast the most important meal of the day. What you eat for breakfast pretty well determines

how you feel the rest of the day." Too much carbohydrate and not enough protein and bulk are common errors in the diet that usually produce a lack of energy later in the day and cause people to indulge in stimulants, such as coffee and soft drinks containing caffeine. "Caffeine has differing effects on people", continues Dr. Campbell, "but none of them aid the emotional stability and calmness you need to deal effectively with your teenager."

What a difference it makes when we can get up in the morning feeling alive and capable of accepting a new day's challenges! Most people today are leading tremendously busy, stress-filled lives - a very good reason for making sure that bodies and minds are receiving the nutrients they need to cope with these demands.

The ads on TV seem to take it for granted that various aches and pains are a normal part of everyday life. Perhaps because of this we accept less than good health as though that's the way "everybody" feels. To feel alive and alert, with clear heads and a 'get-up and go' feeling is every human beings' rightful heritage. Why should we settle for less? Adults who exercise, who eat foods chosen for good nutrition as well as taste, are better able to live their lives effectively in every dimension - family, work, and play.

No act of kindness
No matter how small
Is ever wasted.

Aesop

If only I may grow;
Firmer, simpler ·
Quieter, warmer.

Dag Hammarskjold

If the day and night are such that you greet them with joy,
and life emits a fragrance like flowers and sweet-scented
herbs—is more starry, more immortal—that is your success.
All nature is your congratulation.

Thoreau

Reading Music

When your child goes to school, or sometimes even before, he learns to read the language he has been speaking for a number of years. We consider this the natural sequence of development. Why then should there be so much controversy over the child who learns to play music before he learns the written symbols for musical language?

I can remember the consternation of a piano teacher whom my mother had chosen to be my first teacher. In the course of the introductory conversation my mother mentioned that I had been playing by ear, picking up tunes that I'd heard her play and some from the radio. With great seriousness the teacher replied, "Thank goodness you're starting her lessons now. If she went on playing by ear without learning to read music it could be a great handicap later on." I don't remember questioning her about that dire prognosis. We thought of her as the expert and her opinion was accepted without question. This outmoded thinking is responsible for the concern over the delay in music reading which is a normal part of Suzuki training.

First of all let me inform you that the number of traditionally trained music students—especially pianists—who are excellent sight-readers of music are very few. Reading music at sight, which is comparable to what we do with language when we pick up a book, is generally a very poorly developed skill.

Many of us don't realize that there was only the crudest form of musical notation in existence until the medieval period. People learned by imitating those with whom they had personal contact. For that reason improvisation and composition were considered in everyone's capability. Musicians were not captives of the printed page, and it was no sin to play "by ear" something you'd heard someone else play. If you have read biographies of well-known performing artists who were prodigies in their day, you will note that most grew up in an atmosphere permeated by music. Mothers or fathers, or both, were either amateur or professional musicians and the children were surrounded by the sound of music. The outcome? They just began to play!

William Primrose, the famous violist, in his autobiography, "Walk on the North side" recounts, "As an infant I often sat on the floor with a wooden stick in each hand—one, of course, represented the violin and the other the bow—and copied my father's movements as he played. When he, relishing my enthusiasm, bought and placed a quartersized violin in my eager hands in 1908, I began at once really to play."

A few years ago I invited a local teacher into my studio to look at a video tape of a program of young Japanese pianists that had been made during our stay in Japan. She had shown some slight interest in knowing what the Suzuki method was all about. I felt that seeing these young children perform so beautifully was an impressive introduction. After a five-year-old girl finished the Gigue of the B Flat Partita by Bach (the last piece in Book IV) I turned off the tape. There was a moment of silence. "Can they read music?" she questioned coldly.

My jaw dropped! Could anyone not be emotionally excited by this child, this infant, reaching such a high level of musical ability? What difference did it make whether she could read? Did that change this exciting experience?

When an infant displays an impressive vocabulary, is able to verbalize thoughts and feelings coherently or memorizes a poem, who discounts that ability by questioning, "Can he read?" Instead, we are delighted by such a display of ability. Where then have we gotten off the track in recognizing the development of musical language?

Reading Music—An Invaluable Skill

Lest you think that we do not consider music reading important, we want to state right here that the preceding paragraphs are presented only to accentuate the validity of Suzuki's mother-tongue method. "Speak first—read later." "Play first—read later."

Just as we consider the reading of language an absolute necessity for the whole human being, so we consider the reading of music a necessity for the musician—professional or amateur.

Two Kinds of Reading

It is important that we clarify here the two kinds of music reading. First: the child is reading music when he knows and can identify musical symbols, names and locations of notes on the staff, kinds of notes and their values, clef signs, time signatures, rests, etc. With this knowledge he should be able to work out and learn new music. Second: a child is 'sight-reading' music when he can look at the musical page and can play what is written there in the proper location with the proper rhythmic structure at the proper tempo. He can literally 'at sight' bring the music to life, translating symbols in the music as conceived by the composer. There is no study involved, except perhaps a superficial 'looking over' what is on the page. It is performed at the moment it is seen. Hence, the term 'sight-reading'. This is the skill we want to develop.

In an introduction to a sight-reading book, Sir Ernest MacMillan has this to say. "While good sight-reading is obviously essential to a would-be-professional-musician, it is no less important to the amateur. Indeed it stands to reason that, when a student has given up the idea of a musical career HIS MAINTAINING OR DROPPING AN INTEREST IN MUSIC AS A HOBBY WILL DEPEND IN ALMOST EXACT PROPORTION ON HIS ABILITY TO READ AT SIGHT. If he has nothing to play but the few pieces he has learned in his days of music study and no time to practice new ones his interest will soon pall, whereas the good sight-reader may keep his interest alive with almost unlimited new material, even though he never brings his playing to a stage of technical excellence fit for public performance." That says in a nutshell exactly what we feel about the place of music reading in the training of young musicians.

Music Reading is a Psycho-Motor Task

In the realm of language it is a natural thing to expect that when one knows the letters of the alphabet, their sounds, and the words that combinations of letters produce, the ability to 'sight-read' will follow. We expect only the beginning reader to struggle with a kind of working-out process—slowly sounding out words, stumbling and hesitating, making not much understandable sense out of what is being

189

read. (I remember lying with David on his bed after dinner when he was in the first grade, listening to him laboriously sound out a new word and then repeat the phrase or sentence to make sense out of it after he knew the word! It was exciting to see the evolution from that stage into the stage of proficiency.)

Yet reading music is different. It involves a physical response to a mental stimulus—a new physical skill. In reading language our responses are already learned. We don't have to teach our vocal chords to make the sounds of the letters and words.

Studies on Reading Music

Robert G. Petzold advanced the idea that effectiveness in music reading is hindered in the early stages of instrumental training because of the concern with developing control over the instrument rather than with the musical notation. He felt that one of the significant problems contributing to poor music reading has been the lack of musical experiences before a student begins to learn to read music.

J. Watson pointed out the need of a music vocabulary by stating, "So in learning to read music as in learning to read language we must build a vocabulary based on direct experience."

What great recommendations for Suzuki training! The Suzuki student has had much direct experience with music before he learns to read the language.

When Do We Begin to Read?

Although we have said in the previous section that many activities can be done that prepare and preview music reading, we do not believe that actual music reading from the page should be done by pianists during the study of Book I. Until the important goals of Book I—focused attention, good posture, position and tone, firm fingers and rhythmic feeling—are well established for that stage of development, reading should not be considered. Generally speaking, we feel that all students need the experience of learning and reviewing all of the pieces of Book I before beginning to read. Exceptions may occur, but I think they are rare. An older child who learns very quickly and has easily formed all the correct attitudes and habits may be considered an exception. It may be feasible to begin reading sooner with a child like this. Our judgment must be based on the accomplishment of the above goals.

If the child begs to begin reading, parents need to explain the reasons for the delay. The desire to read can motivate the child to learn to play!

Your response could be, "Sandy, your teacher wants us to be sure that you are set in all of your good habits before we start looking at the music. If you always pay very good attention and listen to what she says and to what you are doing, if you have good posture, good hand position and firm fingers, if you play with a beautiful tone and good rhythm on all the pieces in Book I, we will be able to begin reading. Let's work on these things as we practice each day and then it won't be long. That will be really exciting, don't you think?"

I agree that the violinist also should not begin to read music until his basic technique is well established. Students usually take all of Book I to learn to play with good posture, a good bow hold, correct left hand position and finger action, and straight, firm bow strokes. This is a place where overlearning is especially needed. Reading music demands so much of the learner that he will not be able to devote much attention to his basic technique. If this technique is not well set, it will deteriorate as he neglects it to learn to read.

Once I taught a college string methods class by rote. These students were wind, brass, and percussion players who were required to learn basic string techniques. The head of the music education department had agreed to allow me to teach the class by the Suzuki method, but had insisted that I should also make the students acquainted with the elementary string methods that were in current use in the public schools. They were to play through several of the beginning books during the semester.

After six weeks of rote instruction to which the class responded enthusiastically, I brought in copies of one of the method books for the students to read through. Before they began to play, I emphasized the importance of maintaining good posture and fine tone.

You ought to have seen the reaction of the class to the introduction of reading! "I'm not ready!" exclaimed a fine clarinetist. "We're not either!" the others protested. "But you already know how to read music," I remonstrated. "What's so difficult?"

"Of course we can read the music! We're just not ready to take any of our attention away from our playing. We still need to watch our bows and our fingers."

This was a conscientious group. They had grown used to working for a good tone and good intonation, and felt that it was impossible to continue to do so if they had to give even a minimum of attention to reading. We finally compromised by alternating rote playing and reading music.

It was surprising how much the tone quality changed for the better each time we returned to rote playing. If combining playing and reading was difficult for these young adult musicians, one can see how difficult it could be for the young beginner whose basic technique is not set.

Getting Ready to Read

During the study of Book I there are many concepts and symbols that can be introduced to the student. Children consider learning these fun, so they can be done during rest periods in practice sessions or at lessons, if the teacher wishes. Your teacher may discuss her ideas about this with you.

Pianists can be introduced to the "high and low", "up and down" concepts of the keyboard, and the names of the keys. They can also learn the names of the notes on the staff, learn the alphabet backwards, recognize rhythmic groups of twos and threes when heard, clap the beat to recognize the durations of quarter, half, whole, and dotted half notes, and learn to recognize clef signs, flats, sharps, etc.

Answer any questions children might ask about how certain things look on the printed page by showing it to them. When the teacher asks for specific attention to some points in the piece . . . accents, crescendos, diminuendos, staccato, etc., point to them on the page during practice at home. Casually comment that they will see these often when they learn to read music.

Practicing Reading

Once the Suzuki student has begun to read music it is necessary to practice it every day as a part of the regular practice period. At first this reading period will be short but gradually it should become twenty minutes to a half hour of the practice session.

Music educator J. Fisher supports daily reading practice with this statement, "Real understanding of musical notation involves consistent day to day attention to the symbols and practice in their use."

We are all aware that "knowing" is not enough to accomplish a skill. It's the "doing", the actual experience using our knowledge, that teaches us to be skillful. The practice of using the musical symbols learned is the deciding factor in becoming an accomplished music reader.

Practice, of course, must be specific to a particular skill. This should be remembered when the time spent on theory and games is considered "reading" exercise. These activities may provide necessary background knowledge but they do not substitute for actual reading experience.

A new skill must be done regularly and often for one to become proficient in it. For that reason music reading practice shouldn't be considered an adjunct to practice but a part of it. Be sure both your child and you understand that.

Sight and Vision—Its Relation to Music Reading

Children are given school eye examinations at regular intervals using the familiar Snellen chart. This chart dates from around the time of the Civil War and was designed mostly to test children's ability to see the school blackboard. This examination measures only visual acuity, or clarity and sharpness of sight. Sight is the mere ability to see, the eye's response to light shining into it. Vision, on the other hand, is the result of the child's ability to interpret and understand the information that comes to him through his eyes. This is a learned process. Children may have 20/20 eye sight or even better and still have critical vision problems that interfere with school work and hence music reading.

A child learns visual skills just as he learns to walk and talk. Children who are restricted in play pens and walkers are prevented from having the crawling and creeping experiences that provide a range of movement and normal development patterns. Children who don't creep long enough or who are restricted in their physical exploration of the environment frequently move into life with a disability. It is a handicap that may never be exposed during physical or eye examinations.

Since a child must first learn to team the two halves of his body together before he can team his two eyes, so he must first learn to control the large gross muscles before he can control the fine muscles of his eyes. For that reason, balance boards, walk rails and jumping boards or trampolines plus crawling and creeping are an important part of vision training.

Here are clues that might indicate a possible need for vision therapy:

1. *Blurred vision, double vision, words running together.*
2. *Reversals when reading—was for saw, on for no, etc.*
3. *Reversals when writing—b for d, p for q, etc.*
4. *Transposition of letters and numbers—12 for 21, etc.*
5. *Loss of place when reading, line to line and word to word.*
6. *Use of finger to maintain place.*
7. *Holding book too close.*
8. *Omitting small words.*
9. *Confusing small words.*
10. *Short attention span.*
11. *Daydreaming in class.*
12. *Poor handwriting.*
13. *Clumsiness on playground or at home.*

If your child's performance is not up to his potential, if verbal ability far exceeds visual learning ability, you can suspect a vision problem. Observations from teachers—or from you—that the child "is lazy", "doesn't try", "could do better if he exerted more effort", point to the possibility of a vision problem. Even surly, hostile or belligerent behavior may be an indication of visual/perception dysfunction.

Optometrists in vision development suggest examination by the age of three so that any problems or lack of development can be found and corrected before school attendance. Of course, it's never too late to try to correct a later discovered problem.

I became interested in this because of observing the great number of students (not Suzuki students but general music students) who had difficulty reading music. The possiblity that vision problems might be causing some of these difficulties intrigued me.

Some astonishing figures will show the prevalence of this handicap. In one study, 1 out of 4 students were shown to have significant reading deficiencies. Seventeen million school children are achieving much below their potential with ten percent so severely handicapped that they are literally unable to learn. The Commission of Education ran a study called Project 100,000 with the U.S. Armed Forces and found 68.2% of the young men fell below grade 7 in reading and academic ability.

If you even slightly suspect your child might need this kind of help, seek out a vision therapist in your area. (For more information write: College of Optometrists in Vision Development: P.O. Box 285, Chula Vista, CA 92012.)

A Good Reading Environment

1. Young children need optimal visibility when beginning to read music. Large notes and symbols and good lighting are absolutely necessary for success.
2. Children show very slow rate of progress in early stages of sensory-motor learning. Knowing this, be very patient and understanding of the long period of time they need for accomplishment.
3. Children must repeat each new learning step many, many times to absorb it. Give them that opportunity. Inspire them to do it. Watch with cheerful feelings and encouragement.
4. Children must make each new step automatic before learning something new. Being aware of this, don't be eager to get on with new things. Be sure the step you're working on is automatic before you begin another.

Keep these things in mind and help your teacher by giving her your observations on the progress your child displays at home. That way you can knowledgeably work together on the reading study schedule.

Parents, Want to Learn to Read Music?

If you don't know how to read music, why not start now? You will be a much more understanding home teacher if you do. There's nothing like learning a new skill to put you in a more empathetic, supportive role with another new learner. Learning something new keeps your n.ind sharp, alert and young! Your child will enjoy and appreciate your efforts, too—both because you are open to doing new things and because it makes for greater understanding between you. Besides, if you try it, you might like it!

Importance of Attitude

Reading music is a complex activity and the supportive attitude of the parent can mean a great deal to the learning student.

Parents' positive help, when needed, is most important at the early stage of reading. Avoid statements like: "You played a wrong note", "That whole line was wrong", "Can't you see the difference between a line and a space note?", "You know that interval! Why did you play a third instead of a second?. . . a D instead of an E?" Allow the child to read the pattern, the line or the phrase without stopping even if he makes mistakes. Then, instead of pointing out and correcting the error, say, "I think you made some changes there. There were some notes different from those that are written. Please play it again. I think you'll see them and play it as written this time." If errors still persist, narrow the field. "There was something different in the second measure." Should the student still not play correctly, question, "What is this note? (interval, kind of note, etc.) What should it be? What did you play?" In this way the student is made aware of his mistakes and learns from them because he has been helped to focus on them and make his own correction.

One teacher said, "The most important thing is learning to read music is believing that you can." Our positive attitudes as parents and teachers can help build that belief in our children.

Encourage Your Child to Read

It is an unpleasant adjustment for some children to return to the feeling of being a beginner again when they start to read music. The familiar routine of listening and being guided by the parent is much more comfortable than having to put forth their own effort to make sense of the printed page.

Yet, as we said before, reading music is a valuable skill for any student. The amateur musician's future with music depends upon it. The professional must have it highly developed or many opportunities are unavailable to him.

There are many highly proficient musical performers whose reading skill is very poor. That is similar to the actor learning to recite Shakespeare beautifully with all meaningful inflection and convincing rhetoric, but being unable to read the daily newspaper or a book on a second grade reading level! The limitations are obvious.

It is not very desirable for a musician to stay in the rote-learning category. Sometimes the student needs to have this lack of options pointed out to him to give him the incentive to make the effort to learn to read. There is always hesitation on venturing into new territory. Help him take the step.

The secret of education
Lies in respecting the student.
                    Emerson

Young Bedrich Smetana, the Bohemian composer, thought the sound of his father's violin was a permanent part of his environment. For recreation in the evenings the family would often make music together. Bedrich was three when his father showed him how to handle a violin and keep time to music. By the time he was four he'd mastered the fundamentals of the violin—at five he started the piano, and at six made his first public appearance.

Your Child's Instrument

Is a Good Piano Necessary for the Beginning Student?

Your four-year-old Nancy is ready to start Suzuki piano lessons. You are eager to have her begin but the purchase of a piano does not have top priority on your acquisition list. "Since pianos are so expensive and we don't really know whether Nancy will continue, let's just get an old used piano that won't cost much," you say. "Later we can invest in a better one after we find out whether she's really interested. The one I found sounds like a piano in the Blue Lounge Bar. The keys keep sticking, and pedals don't work, but we'll get it fixed. It will have to do for now."

You, mother, want to learn to sew and your husband agrees that the purchase of a sewing machine can be considered. "But", he says, "since we don't know whether your interest in sewing will continue, I think we should buy this old 1909 Singer advertised in the paper. I called the owner. She says it runs but is temperamental at times. The stitches are irregular and don't seem to respond to the setting knob. The motor makes a funny noise but we'll get it fixed. It will have to do for now."

Can you imagine that any interest you might have in sewing will be nurtured by a broken down machine? What fine garment could be made by a machine of this kind? At your sewing lessons, you would be shown the intricacies of many creative items, but what happens when you try to duplicate them on your antique machine at home? And how long do you expect your interest to continue under those circumstances?

At Nancy's lessons she will be given guidance and stimulation to play with a beautiful sound. If she has a piano at home on which this is impossible to achieve, what will happen to her interest? Frustration and unpleasant sounds do not provide for continued interest and motivation to learn to play.

We all know that we cannot do any job well if we have inferior tools. A musical instrument is the tool of the musician, young or old. The young musician with a poor instrument will probably not persevere to become an old musician. It just isn't a very enjoyable, satisfying or desirable experience when no amount of careful practice can bring beautiful results.

Choosing a Piano

When your child is beginning lessons and you do not own a piano, or if you are wondering whether your piano is adequate, consult your teacher. It is to her advantage that your child has a good instrument at home. She will be glad to advise you. Sometimes you may find an estate or moving family that is selling a used instrument. In this case, you will really need your teacher's expert advice, plus the advice of a technician who could give you an estimate of the amount of work needed to put the piano in good shape.

In most cities there are piano stores who rent pianos with the agreement that the rental fee will apply to the purchase price should you decide to buy later. This may be your best solution because it provides you access to a decent instrument without your making a sizeable financial commitment at the outset of your child's training.

Musical Instrument Versus Furniture

Try to keep in mind that this piano is to function primarily as a musical instrument and not as a piece of furniture. It is fine if the style of the case and woodgrain compliment your decor, but that should be a secondary consideration. Naturally, if you are going to have it in a living room setting, you are not going to want a monstrosity that looks like it came from Dracula's castle, but if you must make some compromise, let it be in the furniture category, not the instrumental one!

Naturally, it would be nice if every piano student could have a nine-foot concert grand to begin on but this is not feasible, space-wise or financially, for most people. I would like to put thumbs down on the spinet-style piano that has been so popular because its appearance is so 'romantic'. Inasmuch as the sounding board on the spinet is very short, the bass register tones sound like dull 'thuds'. The upright grand is a better choice because the sounding board extends up behind the music rack and gives the lower register more tonal resonance. The baby grand has the best potential but of course its price is much higher than the upright grand.

Care and Maintenance of Your Piano

Your teacher will be glad to refer you to a good piano technician so that you can keep your instrument in good playing condition.

During the winter months a humidifier may be needed because of the heat in the house. A humidistat to measure the humidity in the room may be purchased inexpensively. It is best to keep the humidity level around 40%. In certain areas of the country, as in Tennessee, it is necessary to have a dehumidifier in the summer if the room is not air conditioned. Too much moisture may cause the keys to stick. On the other hand, an atmosphere that is too dry may cause the sounding board to dry out and crack.

It is best to locate the piano on an inside wall because of the ease of maintaining an even temperature there. Care of the instrument should not be the only consideration for its location. Keep in mind that the location of the piano may also affect the child's attitude toward daily practice. If the instrument is stuck down in a far-off corner of the basement away from all normal human interaction, that is not a pleasant environment for practice. Neither should the piano be placed in proximity to the TV set, or a play area. Whenever possible, these factors should be considered.

It is best to have the piano tuned regularly every six months if normal conditions prevail. Remember that the ears we're trying to develop become very sensitive to out-of-tune sounds! Sometimes parents are astounded when the child complains "that note doesn't sound right" when they themselves don't notice any difference at all. This is just another example of the marvelous sensitivity and hearing ability of children.

Since most of the new piano keys are topped with plastic, they don't need as much care as did the ivory keys. (At least we can be happy that pianists are not contributing to the demise of the elephant anymore!) It is still best to keep the piano keys clean with a soft, damp cloth. No soap should be necessary and excessive wetness should be avoided for obvious reasons.

It is true that pianos are a major investment, but with time for investigation and the expert help of your teacher and a technician, you should be able to find an instrument that will satisfy the needs of your child and your budget.

Choosing a String Instrument

Fortunately, finding a suitable small instrument for the beginning string player is not nearly the undertaking parents have with the young pianist. You should follow the guidance of your teacher with regard to the purchase of the small instruments, either new or used. Most teachers are very helpful in this matter. They want your child to have a fine instrument in good condition, and they will help to see that this is so.

When your child arrives at the need for a full-size violin or cello, you will have to continue relying on your teacher's advice. A better instrument will generally be easier for your child to play and will be an aid to the production of a better tone, but there are limits to this. I don't think there's any reason to give a child a violin from which he can draw only a fraction of the quality and quantity of sound it possesses. So much depends on the player. An admirer of Jascha Heifetz exclaimed after a concert, "Mr. Heifetz, your violin has a glorious tone!" Heiftez bent an ear toward the violin resting in its open case. "I don't hear anything", he replied.

At the full-size stage, I think an instrument should be bought for its tone and appearance rather than the name of the maker. Unfortunately, as one moves to a better instrument to get an appreciable difference in the tone quality, one has to spend quite a bit more money.

Some children are motivated to practice more by the fact that they have just acquired a new (to them) instrument. Some may even feel obligated to practice more when they know there has been a considerable outlay of family funds for their instrument!

I think the time to consider a major investment for a string instrument is at college entrance. The most important factors influencing the price of the instrument would of course be the family's finances and the serious intent of the student. I remember being shown a magnificent violin, worth at least $30,000, that had been given to a high school girl of indifferent ability. Oh, she was thrilled by its value but was unable to appreciate its tonal possibilities because she could not produce a good tone on the instrument. I didn't feel so badly later after I heard that the violin was given her by her multimillionaire grandfather. Who knows, perhaps today she is practicing like a fiend!

Choosing a Bow

Small bows, like the small instruments, are fairly standardized in quality and price. Your child will most probably have gotten his first bow with the violin, and will continue to get a bow with each larger-size violin. Even the first full-size violin may come with a bow and case.

When your teacher feels that your child should have a better bow, follow her guidance if family finances permit. As the student becomes more advanced, the bow he uses becomes more important. A bad bow may have a strong negative effect on a student's growth, more than most parents realize. I see more hopeless bows than I do hopeless violins!

Care and Maintenance of String Instruments

When your child receives his first instrument, your teacher will give both of you instructions regarding care and maintenance of the violin and bow. Your child should form the habit of taking great care of these from the beginning. This is part of the preparation for practice and lessons. Periodically, you should ask your teacher to let you know how the violin and bow are faring. Are you putting enough rosin, or too much, on the bow? Does the bow need rehairing? Should you replace the strings? Is the bridge all right? We teachers need to be reminded of these things. We know better, but sometimes we forget to keep a constant check on these matters.

Parents need to know that even with the best of care, under normal use string instruments need adjustments and repairs. With fine instruments, this may run into several hundreds of dollars at times, but not every year. String players usually spend more money keeping fine old instruments maintained than they do modern instruments, although these also suffer from lack of attention over a period of time.

Prices

You may be disappointed that there are no price guidelines given here. If we were to do so, our information would be out of date by the time this book is printed. We remember, with nostalgia, buying a fine half-size violin in Matsumoto for Judith in 1968 for $28! And that included bow and case. In this era of rising prices, parents whose children study string instruments may be consoled by the fact that their instruments, if well-cared for, are also appreciating in value!

Where there is great love
There are always miracles.

Willa Cather

"From the day I was born I heard music", so said Serge Prokofiev, the famous Russian composer pianist. As soon as he could balance himself on the piano stool next to his mother, she let him be a part of her daily practice. Soon she began to give him short lessons—never exceeding twenty minutes. When he was five and a half he picked out the notes of his first tunes, playing them over and over again.

Finding and Choosing a Teacher

During the past few years our mailbox has been the recipient of many letters from anxious parents who are moving to a new area, or from equally anxious Suzuki teachers whose students are moving. Both parents and teachers want to be sure that their students find a competent Suzuki teacher.

Unless we've had the opportunity to work with a teacher personally, or have heard or worked with his students, or know a close colleague who has had that opportunity and recommends him on that basis, we find it difficult to give a recommendation that is of much value. We can only suggest that those inquiring search the directory of the Suzuki Association of the Americas for names of teachers in the new location, or write the SAA for the files on teachers in the area. You should do the same. If the teachers have registered their work with the SAA, you will be able to see what kind of training and experience they have had. If you have a choice of teachers, no matter what training and experience is indicated, you will want to observe the teachers at work before you decide who might be the best for your child.

Since Suzuki teachers should be accustomed to having observers during lessons, the process should not be too difficult. Call each teacher, explain that you are interested in the Suzuki method for your child and that you and your child would like to attend some lessons and programs. Our advice to parents has been: if a teacher doesn't allow observation visits, cross that teacher off your list.

When you attend the lessons of a prospective teacher, observe the relationships between teacher and child, and teacher and parent. Does the teacher make sure that the parent knows what the goals are for home practice? Is the atmosphere pleasant and relaxed? Does the teacher expect and receive respectful attention? Is there a good balance between concentrated work and good humor? Are the teacher's comments supportive and encouraging even when necessary corrections are made? Does the teacher show a grasp of the basic technical problems, and demonstrate how they can be solved? To questions such as these, add prerequisites important to you. Remember that the game-playing good-humored, entertaining teacher might not be the best choice unless these qualities are balanced by the expertise of a well-trained teaching musician.

Don't be fooled into believing that 'anyone can teach Suzuki'. It's fine if one loves children, praises and encourages them, provides listening opportunities and uses the Suzuki repertory, but the teacher must also have knowledge of the technique of the instrument. I have had individuals tell me that they thought they could teach their own childen even though they had had little or no musical background. They felt that buying the books and combining the repertory with the Suzuki philosophy that they already knew was all that was necessary.

How would you feel if your child's math teacher walked into the classroom and announced, "Look, kids, this is going to be a great year. I really don't know anything about math . . . I mean I never studied it beyond grade school, but I have a book, and I'll study it along with you". You'd probably call the school office immediately to find out why they had employed a teacher with no math background or expertise to teach math to your child.

You should be just as concerned that your child have a knowledgeable, competent musician as a teacher. It will make a great deal of difference in the development of her abilities. Whether she develops her ability according to her potential or becomes what my husband calls a 'terminal case' depends upon your teacher's expertise. There is no substitute for a competent musician who has embraced the Suzuki approach to musical training. This kind of teacher has the necessary broad background that you should want your child to be given. Don't settle for less. It's an investment that will bring worthwhile results.

If you are moving into an area where there is no Suzuki teacher listed in the SAA directory, that doesn't mean that no Suzuki teacher exists there. It might mean that the teacher has not yet joined SAA, has not kept up membership, or is just a loner! Talk to parents, look in the phone directory, question the music teacher in your child's school, or call the local music stores. If after all that, no names have turned up, investigate the surrounding towns or cities. Many parents drive long distances to provide a teacher for their children. At one time families came from Illinois, Kentucky, Georgia, and North Carolina to our studio in Knoxville.

If your search reaches a dead end, rethink your problem. If your child has finished Book 2 and is reading music adequately for that stage of development, you are in good shape. You can look for a competent teacher who is sympathetic and open to the Suzuki concepts. This is very important! Some traditional teachers seem to be hell-bent on proving the Suzuki approach won't and can't work. If you team up with such a teacher inadvertently, head for the nearest door immediately. That kind of relationship can only end in unhappiness for you and your child. If your child is not yet reading and you want her to continue study in the Suzuki style, you might try to interest a resident, reputable, well-trained teacher to study and adopt Suzuki principles with your child.

Changing Teachers

Some parents feel that because their child's teacher is particularly adept at working with very young children, that same teacher cannot teach advanced literature. There is no basis for such an assumption. Rather, the teacher's training and experience will have a great bearing on his being successful with teaching your child on an advanced level. It is not necessary for the teacher to have all of the literature under his fingers ready for performance, but it is extremely helpful if the teacher has played the music your child is to study, or music of comparable difficulty.

The most advanced performer in the community, however, may not be the best teacher for your child. He may not be able to communicate well, may not have a supportive personality, and may not be able to diagnose your child's particular problems and guide her accordingly.

A case like the following is unfortunate. An excellent Suzuki teacher, who had yet not had any students past Book VIII, had taught a young girl to play very well in Book VI. A nearby college brought in a nationally-known violinist to perform a recital and conduct a weekend of master classes for students of all ages. This particular girl made a great impression him. "Your daughter plays beautifully," he said to her mother. "May I suggest to you that she be given the best instruction available in this area?" No mention was made of the superior instruction that had brought this girl to that position of excellence!

The mother, gathering that he was recommending a new teacher, dropped the Suzuki teacher at once, and enrolled her daughter with the violin teacher at that college who was known as a fine performer but was not generally regarded by his peers as a good teacher.

This mother's precipitate action hurt the Suzuki teacher's reputation with the other parents. They began to think that she was not capable of teaching on a more advanced level. And the little girl floundered under her new instructor who was particularly inept at working with a young, precocious child. In this case, I knew the capabilities of the Suzuki teacher, and felt that it would have been better for all concerned if the girl had remained with her teacher who was certainly qualified to teach the little girl through Book X.

I had a delightful eleven-year-old girl in a master class at an institute this summer. She played beautifully and responded well but seemed depressed about something. I asked her teacher if she knew what was bothering her. "Yes, I know, and it depresses me too," said the teacher. "Her father thinks she's too good to continue as a Suzuki student, so he's starting her with another teacher after this institute. He let her attend it as her farewell to the Suzuki world. She still cries when she thinks of losing her association with her friends at group lessons, and also when she thinks of stopping her lessons with me. I told her she could come to group lessons whenever she wanted, that she would always be welcome. Still, she's pretty upset."

This was another case in which the teacher happened to be well qualified for continuing the child's musical education. I felt that the change of teachers could have been justifiably and profitably delayed for two or three years. If the girl had been with her Suzuki teacher for a number of years, which she had not, the teacher's effectiveness might have diminished. Length of study with one teacher may be a factor contributing to the desirability of change, but again, it may not.

I am not suggesting that the child should not change teachers under any circumstances, but that such a change should be well thought out. If you are truly convinced that your child has outgrown her teacher, and you have arrived at that conclusion after much deliberation, try to effect the change as smoothly and tactfully as possible. If you or your child, however, are suffering from a personality conflict with your child's teacher, and you don't think there's much chance of change for the better, of course you should terminate the relationship without undue delay.

In all cases involving a change of teachers, I advise parents to weigh as objectively as possible all the pros and cons of the situation before taking any action. A hasty decision should be avoided.

Institute Environment

Parents often come away from institutes confused about the true worth of their child's teacher. Institute directors try their best to hire fine teachers but this doesn't mean that your teacher is automatically inferior to all of the institute teachers. If you have seen, at an institute, teaching that seems to you superior to that of your teacher's, and you feel that your teacher is capable of equalling it, you might discuss this privately with your teacher. If you hear remarks that contradict the way your child has been taught, try to talk to the institute teacher about it, and also discuss it with your teacher. You may still be confused but at least you have tried to clarify the situation. Your teacher may be wrong, the institute teacher may be wrong, or they may both be right, since, even in Suzuki teaching, many paths may lead to Rome. Don't assume without question that your teacher is wrong.

Under no circumstances should you automatically accept, as Bill has said, the fact that your home teacher is deficient because of what you observe at institutes or workshops. Unless you are a well-schooled instrumentalist yourself, you will have to question, study, and spend time and effort to wisely evaluate your situation before forming an opinion or taking an action.

A situation was called to my attention recently by an excellent teacher, a well-qualified teacher trainer, a teacher whose work I have admired for some time, who had sent some of her students to a summer institute. The institute teacher had questioned the parent about who the child's home teacher was, then made some deprecating remark about the quality of teaching and actually said, "She's been taught all wrong!" This, in front of the student as well as those observing! Naturally, the parent went home, told the teacher they were quitting and recited the above encounter as the reason.

Of course, first of all, no matter what the status of the student's performance, no temporary institute teacher ethically has a right to demolish the reputation of the home teacher. How does he know what that child has been told at home and how many times it has been repeated with no results?! The correct procedure would be to talk to the mother alone after class, question her, and then perhaps make suggestions or merely understand the differences. From that a positive outcome might have resulted. If this was an erroneous evaluation, which it must have been in this case, we can only suspect that the institute teacher saw validity in only his way of teaching and was not open to the thought that there could be variations of any kind. This is sometimes dangerous thinking and you would be wise to approach this kind of encounter with caution. Bolting to another teacher is not the answer . . . the grass is not always greener!

Fun and Games or Joy and Enthusiasm

I've heard parents complain that institute teachers are more entertaining than the teacher at home. Parents should realize the situation confronting the institute teacher. Because of the difficulty of making much impact on a child in four or five fifteen-minute lessons, and because there are often observers in the room, he may resort to entertaining the child and parent with games. These games may be all right in themselves, but not at all suitable as a steady diet week after week and would not be used by that institute teacher with his own students at home. We remember being surprised to see Suzuki using so few games with his private students.

There is a prevalent but mistaken idea circulating in our Western adaptation of the Suzuki method that Suzuki training has game playing and 'fun' activity as its central core. We are seeing more and more efforts being focused on the production of games to cover every aspect of music learning.

Somewhere along the line our Western minds have been led to believe that all work and learning must be sugar-coated or disguised—kind of like a bitter pill that must be swallowed but is fundamentally good for you. Only if we camouflage learning will it be accepted, we are saying.

One teacher who watched video tapes of some Japanese piano lessons commented, "There certainly doesn't seem to be much fun involved. They just seem to be constantly working hard." That's true, I suppose, if you consider all work as drudgery and discount the joy of accomplishment. It is true that private lessons in Japan are not made up of 'fun and games'. If a creative teacher finds a way to approach a problem with a kind of game, he will certainly use it. Suzuki himself is quite a playful fellow and will often entertain with creative, functional games at group lessons, but private (one on one) lessons are basically working periods devoid of 'entertainment' for entertainment's sake. The secret of education, Suzuki says, is to approach music or any learning without a strict, formal attitude, but with joy and enthusiasm from the teacher. Then the child will 'catch' that joyful spirit and will develop a skill that will bring him happiness.

When you are evaluating a teacher, look for loving care of the child coupled with high standards for every level of performance. Your child should be consistently challenged to produce the best of which she is capable. It is possible for this to be done in an atmosphere of love and encouragement.

One kind word
    Can warm
        Three winter months.
            Japanese Proverb

Be like the bird
    That pausing in her flight
Awhile on boughs too slight,
    Feels them give way beneath her
And yet sings,
    Knowing that she has wings.
                        Victor Hugo

The ends of the earth stand in awe at the sight of your
wonders, the lands of sunrise and sunset you fill with your joy!
                        Psalm 65

Orchestral Experience

School Orchestras

What should you do when your Suzuki-trained violinist or cellist enters the fourth grade and wants to join the orchestra and play with her friends, or when the school orchestra director asks your child to join? (Most public school programs start at the fourth grade.)

I think the first thing you should do is to discuss the whole subject, pros and cons, with your child's Suzuki teacher. If your teacher knows the public school string teacher or knows of his work and personality, you are fortunate. If not, either of you can inquire about the quality of the program and the instructor. Ask other parents, other music teachers, attend the orchestra's programs, or ask to look in on a class. More and more public school string teachers are Suzuki-oriented and have their own programs in earlier grades. Your child might then have no problem with adaptation.

You must realize that no matter how competent the string teacher may be, it is still very difficult to teach, in the same class, beginners and youngsters who've had several years of Suzuki training. The string teacher is in a far worse situation than the first grade teacher whose entering class contains children who already read well. That teacher can give separate reading assignments and the readers can progress at different rates, but the orchestra players are all supposed to play the same thing at the same time!

Some public school teachers become very defensive when confronted with such a situation. They are afraid of the Suzuki student becoming bored, and possibly disruptive, or acting in an arrogant manner toward the beginners. Frankly, I think it's almost unimagineable that a child who has had several years of study would not become bored sitting in a class with youngsters who were being taught to play their very first notes! If your child has had no previous reading experience, reading the notes might occupy her for some time, but since reading progresses very slowly at the beginning, this might not prove enough of a challenge.

You might discuss these possible alternatives with your teacher and the school teacher:

1) your child be placed in the more advanced orchestra if she, as a fourth grader, doesn't feel out of place playing with sixth graders.

2) your child attend only those classes immediately prior to a concert.

3) your child volunteer to play viola so that she will also be, in a sense, a beginner. Knowledge of the viola clef will be very helpful later.

If none of these are acceptable to all concerned, you might want to keep your child out of the orchestral program until the sixth grade when the other youngsters have become fairly proficient. This is often the best solution. If you do decide on this course, don't let your child join a more advanced orchestra without sufficient music-reading preparation.

Music Reading Important

Our son, Tim, coming back from studying with Suzuki in Japan, went into a junior high orchestra without any previous orchestral experience and with very little training in music reading. He had been almost nine when he started studying violin in our then-new Suzuki program. Although he listened to the recordings faithfully, he did use the music to help learn the fingerings and bowings. I mistakenly thought he was developing the ability to read music, and had decided to start reading instruction at the level of Book IV. At that time we left for Japan and the whole business was postponed.

Tim was shocked when he auditioned for seating in the school orchestra. Everyone seemed to know that he was the best violinist in the school, but the orchestra director, after hearing his attempts to sight read music, put him on the last stand of the third violins! (I really felt and still feel guilty about this, but it did make me keenly conscious of the student's need for everyday experience in reading.)

Tim was concertmaster of the orchestra by Christmas. When I told him I was sorry that I had not prepared him earlier, he said, "Well, anyway, it's a lot easier to learn to read music than it is to learn to play the violin."

Be sure your teacher helps your child develop sight reading skills. I don't mean just acquiring theoretical knowledge, nor learning a new piece from the music, but actually developing the ability to sight read music she has never heard. Group lessons provide opportunities for more advanced students to sight read in an ensemble setting, and should be used for that purpose in addition to rehearsing Suzuki literature in unison, or teaching supplementary material using music. Also, the student should be sight reading material daily at home. Etudes are fine for this purpose.

If your child goes into the beginning orchestra, indoctrinate her with the proper attitude. She shouldn't feel superior to a classmate who is a beginner at age nine or ten, who isn't studying privately, and if she does practice at home, practices without parental help!

You may be concerned that your child, playing with beginners in a group situation, will be exposed to a great deal of really bad intonation and will lose her own sensitivity to correct intonation. Being subjected to bad intonation may be painful, but shouldn't be detrimental if the teacher keeps the child's attention on intonation in her own practice. The student should be careful to keep her reaction to bad intonation to herself, or quickly become the most unpopular student in the orchestra!

Despite all of the problems mentioned above, I feel that there can be many advantages to the student's participation in the school orchestra and that the disadvantages can be averted or minimized. School orchestras provide students pleasant sociability with boys and girls in their own school who have similar interests and may provide some exciting musical experiences that are highly motivational. Through affiliation with school orchestras, the student will have the opportunity to participate in music festivals, solo and ensemble competitions, and regional and all-state honors orchestras. The regional and all-state orchestras are especially attractive in that they may provide your student the thrill of playing, for the first time, major compositions in an orchestra with a very large string section. These orchestras usually rehearse intensively for only a few days before a concert. The students are given the music well in advance.

Youth Orchestras

In this category I'm placing all of the orchestras, no matter who sponsors them, that draw their personnel from more than one school and rehearse on a regular basis. Players are usually accepted by audition. These orchestras usually play music more difficult than the school orchestras since they have a bigger pool of players from which to draw their members. Their membership commonly consists of the better players from a number of school orchestras.

Parents often take pride in their children getting into youth orchestras at an early age, but getting in one of these orchestras too early may be detrimental to the child's musical development. Occasionally the conductor or someone managing the youth orchestra will approach you or your child directly and invite her to play in the orchestra. This is flattering, but I would respond by thanking the person and saying that I wanted to discuss the matter with my child's teacher. The teacher will know or should find out what kind of orchestral training the student would be getting in the youth orchestra, and whether your child is ready for that kind of experience. I wouldn't be writing all of this about youth orchestras if I hadn't had personal experience in this field and if I hadn't heard so many Suzuki teachers lament the fact that their fine students often got too heavily involved in orchestras too early.

Parents must realize that it's very difficult for a string player to hear what she's doing in a large orchestra. Too much orchestral playing too soon may cause your child's basic technique to deteriorate. I feel that youth orchestras should be the province of high school students to whom the social aspect is most helpful, and who are mature enough to withstand certain disadvantageous aspects that may arise.

For instance, youth orchestra directors, and sometimes school orchestra directors, may program music that is far too difficult for many of the string players. "Oh well, the difficult string passages will all be covered by the brass anyway", is a line of reasoning one often encounters. This kind of thinking doesn't help the youthful string player's feeling of self-worth or her integrity as a member of the orchestra. Students are sometimes bewildered when they hear loud applause for their orchestral performances when they know that only two or three of the players in their sections could even come close to playing the part correctly. They don't realize that the audience actually couldn't hear all of the mistakes and forgave the ones they did hear because "they were just kids playing". Suzuki students who have been challenged to play as well in groups as they do as soloists find this particularly disturbing.

It is true that many of the difficult string passages are covered up by the brass and percussion. Experienced players know in advance which passages won't be heard and so they go easy on practicing those passages. They know how to 'fake', how to make a reasonable stab at playing the passage without damaging the effect of the whole. This 'cover' provided by the other sections of the orchestra enables many non-professional and semi-professional orchestras to perform acceptably music that is too difficult for many of their string players. However, in top professional orchestras, all of the string players are expected to play all of the notes that it is humanly possible to play. In fact, professional orchestras require string players who audition to play some of the most difficult passages from the orchestral literature. Of course, at these solo auditions there is no 'cover' whatsoever!

If your child is complaining that the music is far too difficult for her, you and she should talk with her teacher. The teacher may not be in any position to make suggestions regarding programming to the orchestra director (most conductors regard this as their exclusive province), although some teachers have been known to warn conductors that if they continue to program music the teacher feels is far too difficult for his students, he may encourage the parents to withdraw their children from the orchestra.

Studying Orchestral Music

No matter if the music is difficult or easy, your child should be in the habit of showing her teacher all of the orchestral music she is playing. The teacher should be asked to incorporate into the lesson orchestral parts for which the child would benefit by the teacher's assistance. Some teachers are understandably reluctant to spend time on orchestral parts, but I feel that if the student is going to play the music anyway, and often with many repetitions, it's better for the teacher to provide guidance so that the student won't be playing incorrectly. Even simple orchestra parts may present problems, often in bowing, that the student has not encountered in the Suzuki literature.

If it's just an occasional piece that contains passages that are really too difficult for your child at that time, your teacher can help the child 'fake' the passages. As I said above, this is an important part of orchestral experience.

If teachers are encouraged to look at orchestral music with a fresh eye, and ask themselves, "How can I make this easy for my student?", they may come up with new fingerings that make the music much easier to play. We teachers need to be reminded of this: what may be the best for us might not be the best for our students at their level. I used to give fingerings that I liked, then I began to look at the music with the goal of finding the easiest fingering possible for my students. With that kind of approach I came upon some innovative fingerings that made the music much easier. Oftentimes, the choice of fingering may be the determining factor in whether or not the child can play the passage.

I know how crowded the lesson can become if time is devoted to orchestra parts, but I put other material aside if the student really needs help. I remember preparing Missy for an audition for the all-state orchestra. The music included the finale of the Shostako-vitch Fifth Symphony which was quite difficult for her but not impossible. I dispensed with all of the other music she was studying so that we could go over the Shostakovitch with careful attention to details. She practiced the part as carefully as she had her solo work. Missy was striving to be concert mistress, and did succeed in getting the second chair even though she had had very little orchestral experience. She gained appreciably from the time we spent on that music. I used the material to develop her technique. Would it have been better if I had continued to cover only her solo pieces in the lessons, and left her to fend for herself with the Shostakovitch? I believe that a sloppy performance in orchestra would have damaged her technique as well as her morale.

ORCHESTRAL EXPERIENCE

Advanced Student

What if your child progresses so rapidly that she is very far ahead of all the other players in the area? Should she enter or remain in the school or youth orchestra if the music is far too simple for her? It may be obvious that she is wasting her time insofar as her own development is concerned, and yet you and she may feel that she has a responsibility to participate in the musical scene of the community. This is a difficult decision to make. If the student is interested in becoming a professional musician, it would probably be better for her to give top priority to her own development, and go to an orchestral camp in the summer for a higher-level orchestral experience.

Auditions for Seating

Discrimination against Suzuki students, taking place at auditions for seating in orchestras, used to be fairly common and still surfaces occasionally. Children should be prepared for the human element that is present in these decisions. Unfairness, favoritism, and discrimination are hard for any child to take, but even more difficult for the Suzuki child who has been trained in a loving, protective, noncompetitive environment. We parents need to be sensitive to our children's feelings and give them the support they need when and if difficulties arise.

No matter how hard one tries to explain to students that auditions for seating may produce some unusual results, it is still quite a shock to the students to see a player whom everyone knows is inferior sitting in the first chair. A girl we knew was complaining to her father about an obvious injustice in seating. "Daddy, it's just not fair!" Her father replied, "Carol, whoever said that life was fair?"

Orchestras Provide Motivation

I hope that your child will have many pleasant experiences in orchestra. Playing a symphony by Tchaikowsky, Beethoven, or Brahms can be very exciting, and playing that symphony with one's friends even more so. Orchestras can provide marvelous motivation, and often do at a time when the student really needs it. Remember, Suzuki initiated his group lessons to provide motivation from the thrill of performance with a large group.

Parents have told us that their children would have dropped the violin or cello if it had not been for the stimulation given by their orchestra. If your child's teacher recommends a particular kind of orchestral experience for her, you should try your best to get her in that orchestra and then give her all the support she needs to continue. You should feel fortunate if fine orchestral experience is within the reach of your son or daughter! As Suzuki says, "Your child will benefit by contact with the minds of the great composers through their music."

May the blessing of light be on you —
Light without and light within.

Old Irish Blessing

Nothing is worth more than this day.

Goethe

No love or friendship can ever cross our path
Without affecting us in some way forever.

Francois Mauriac

Competition—Contests

Competition

"Struggle to win over others" and "a contest between rivals" are the phrases used by Webster to define competition. It is obvious that these phrases are out of place in the Suzuki milieu which de-emphasizes competition as a means to motivate children to practice. Rather, Suzuki hopes that children will be motivated by hearing fine performances of older children and by wanting to play the beautiful pieces that lie ahead.

"How beautifully Mikiko plays! I want to play like she does. I must practice hard so that I will be able to play that well." "That Bach Double Concerto sounds so exciting! I can hardly wait until I play it!" These are the remarks Suzuki likes to hear from children.

Suzuki believes that children benefit from an environment in which they are motivated to play the same music together. His desire is that the environment will be one of contagious enthusiasm. This is one of the reasons his program offers so many opportunities for children and parents to observe the work of other children. Group lessons, frequent solo recitals, and observations of others' lessons are offered to create stimulation but there can be a negative side when parents and children, seeing one child progressing more rapidly than another, are demoralized rather than stimulated. It is often this constant comparative evaluation that causes otherwise understanding parents to push their children ahead and seek a quantitative goal rather than a qualitative one — how many pieces are played rather than how *well* they are played.

We need to remind our children regularly that the proper goal is to play every piece as well as possible as one progresses, and not to race sloppily through as many pieces as possible in the shortest time. Suzuki calls this the "horse-race mentality"!

Often children meeting for the first time at a workshop or institute will ask each other, "What is your last piece?" "I'm in Book IV", is a reply that may demoralize a child who may be much older and yet is

223

only playing through Book III. The first question is never followed up, nor is additional information ever given. I've never yet heard a child say, "I'm in Book IV but I have a lot of problems to overcome", and then enumerate his shortcomings!

Remember! Different Rates of Maturation

In order to offset a possible negative reaction to our observations of other children's progress, we parents need to remind ourselves continually that all children have a different rate of maturation in all fields of endeavor. We also need to ask ourselves questions such as these:

Does my child practice as much and as well as possible?

Does our family life style help him to practice regularly?

Have I been the most helpful home teacher?

Am I willing to give more of my time and energy to help John progress as fast as the other children?

Is my family life more complicated than Mrs. Jones's whose only child progresses so rapidly?

Am I willing to admit that my priorities are different from Mrs. Smiths?

Am I proud of John's interests in many things, but am not happy to settle for less than the best in music even though he cannot spend enough time practicing because of so many other activities?

Can I be satisfied that Susan is making fine progress and enjoying her violin even though she's not one of the best students?

Ambivalence

Even if we have decided that our child's musical development is not one of our top priorities, it is still not easy at times to watch other children move ahead of ours.

When I watched David play soccer, I used to be bothered by two boys who were more skillful players. Even when I found that they spent hours practicing in their back yard, had started playing at age five, and that their father loved soccer, watched it on TV and talked soccer to his children much of the time, I still had a hard time when I watched a game. I liked soccer, was glad that David was playing well and improving, but I would still have liked David to have been the top man on the team even though he spent little time practicing, and didn't have my wholehearted commitment of time, energy and enthusiasm.

I had to face my own irrational attitude when I realized that I was like many of the parents I was exhorting to work more with their children. I liked our children to participate in sports but at the same time wanted their participation to be 'reasonable'. Yet at game time I forgot all this and wanted them to be the best!

Secure and Free

In our chapter on "Sibling Rivalry" we discussed the ever-present competition in daily family life. There is also competition in school, in sports, even in social situations, so we can't avoid it no matter what we do. For the child who feels secure in the love and respect of his parents, these forces need not be destructive.

Joy in the Accomplishments of Others

So often in Japan, parents attending group or private lessons would applaud someone else's child when he gave a good performance. Even in the class of teacher trainees at the Institute, students would show delight when another student succeeded in playing well. There was open rejoicing at the success of others.

How difficult, but how wonderful, if a parent can honestly show delight in another child's accomplishment even when that child is surpassing his own. The child has the opportunity to learn a very important lesson from this. "I can rejoice in other's achievements. If I am giving my best efforts to what I am doing, their accomplishments are not a threat to me."

Our aim, as parents and teachers, is to give our children such security in our love, that the competititon present in our social structure will not intimidate them but will be considered as just another life experience.

Contests

In Suzuki's autobiography, he mentions his first very young student, Toshiyo Eto, as having won a contest at age eleven. After Suzuki started his Talent Education program at the end of World War II, however, there are no references to his entering students in contests in Japan. A number of people have criticized Suzuki in this matter, saying that it would have helped the entire movement had he let the 'mainstream' musical world see how magnificently talent was being developed in his program. This may be so, but it would have been inconsistent with Suzuki's statement that he was not trying to produce professional violinists, but rather trying to enrich the lives of many children by developing their capabilities. Suzuki has never encouraged the use of contests and competition as a motivating force in Talent Education.

Contests, however, are a way of life in the professional musical world. It seems that students seeking a professional performance career benefit by having participated in and won a number of contests, but I still think it is better if children do not enter contests too early. They can be very emotionally disturbing. A student can win one contest and not even place in the next. Judges vary in their likes and dislikes.

Early participation in contests should be limited to those contests in which all students are given ratings in categories: I, or Superior, II, or Excellent, etc. Theoretically all students entering could get in the I category. A competition in which only one person gets first place, one gets second, etc., is often more detrimental than developmental. In the first type of contest, the student is usually given constructive comments by the clinician which can be very helpful to the student and teacher.

Contests may provide strong motivation in some children without producing any detrimental side effects. There are children who relish the excitement of a contest. These children are usually those who have practiced long and well and who have confidence in their ability to succeed. Other children may find the anxiety built up in anticipation of a contest neither helpful nor desirable. Even if your child enters only the rating type of contest, be prepared for circumstances you cannot control and give him plenty of encouragement and support if there is a disappointing outcome.

I remember vividly an unhappy experience with a rating contest in my childhood. I was in seventh grade and had been studying with an excellent teacher whom I loved and respected. Virginia Hardacre not only had a personality that radiated enthusiasm and love of music, but she also encouraged her students to listen to recordings of the works they were learning . . . pre Suzuki! I had studied long and hard on the Scherzo in B Flat Minor, by Chopin and had listened to a recording many, many times, absorbing the style and tempo. Although written in 3/4 time, this piece is felt in one beat to the measure as most scherzi are. I had practiced long hours so that I could play it at the proper tempo.

I was involved in a series of contests constructed on a district, state, and national level. If a student received a I rating in the district contest, he went on to the state level. A I rating in the state meant going on to the national. After playing in the district contest I was elated! The clinician, or judge, as we called her, had welcome words of praise and encouragement, so with confidence I went on to the state level. The performance there went very well, and I looked with anticipation at the posted list, sure that my name would be in the I category. It wasn't there!

I hurried to pick up my critique sheet and read, "You play this piece much too fast! It is written in 3/4 time. Don't play it as though it were one beat per measure." I fought back tears of frustration and disappointment. My teacher was incredulous. She investigated the credentials of the clinician and found that he was a band director and wind player. He simply did not know this literature. There obviously were no qualified pianists available for the position, so someone in the vicinity was drafted. Even though I realized the circumstances I could not help but feel "unfaired" against! It is an incident that is still very vivid in my memory . . . yet I don't spend any emotional energy resenting the experience. Because of the loving support of my mother and teacher it was not a devastating one.

Naturally we don't want to shield our children from all risk of disappointment or failure. It is only through varied life experiences that human potential is developed, character is built and maturation accomplished. If a child is secure in the unconditional love surround-

ing him and is not dependent on "being the best" to assure him a sense of self-worth, all of these experiences can be growth producing. Results can then be accepted without the accompaniment of self-doubt. We should help children evaluate the situation . . . not judge themselves. . . . "That clinician was not knowledgeable. He should not have been in that position. His comments did not reflect on my capabilities."

Weigh your child's resiliency, his confidence and his ability to grow with success and learn from defeat. Then when he enters contests or competitions of any kind, support him, guide him, and love him through it all.

Life-Enriching Benefits

Through his "mother-tongue" method Suzuki has committed himself to the happiness of all children, not just fostering musical sensitivity and performing ability, but fine character and sensitive natures. In articles and speeches throughout the world he repeats again and again that adults should appreciate the privilege of helping their children to become "fine human beings with beautiful harmonious minds and high sensitivity."

Suzuki's passionate conviction that all children possess the potential to be trained to acquire superior abilities is obvious in all he says and does. This is his leitmotif, a refrain he never tires of repeating to all who will listen. I believe that the cornerstone of all his success is his ability to convince so many parents of the superior innate potential their children possess.

Self-Concept—Future Success

There are many benefits for both child and parent in the study of music by the Suzuki approach. Robert Singer, prominent American sports psychologist, wrote, "Enriched and varied early childhood experience is a factor leading to the probability of success in a wide range of undertakings." Margaret Robb, authority on motor-skill acquisition, stated, "When a person is successful in learning a skill, his self-concept is enhanced because of his mastery over the task." Again, Singer writes, "Early successes are important to motivation. Satisfaction achieved elevates the level of performance which in turn increases the probability of better performance output." Dr. James Dobson in his book "Hide or Seek" speaks about the need for developing skills early in childhood so that the child will face his teenage years with what he calls "compensatory" skills, skills that give him a feeling of self-worth during difficult growing years. All of these experts support Suzuki's program for children.

Capacity, Enthusiasm and Respect for Work

When we lived in Matsumoto, Billy, then six, went to the first grade at the Genshi School near our home and near Suzuki's Institute. The Japanese teachers there were anxious to talk with us about American schools. One day we were invited to visit the school for a long informal exchange of information. During the discussion a few of the teachers mentioned some Genshi School students who were studying in Suzuki's program, or had graduated from the kindergarten at the Institute. They said that Suzuki students exhibited a great capacity and enthusiasm for work, also a level of concentration far above average. American and other non-Japanese parents have noticed these same attributes in their Suzuki-trained children.

Concentration

The ability to focus the mind, or concentrate, is a great asset in any and all activity. Using music as a vehicle for its development from an early age is ingenious. Almost without our realizing it Suzuki training fosters this growth.

Suzuki talks about the growth of the span of concentration. "When the small child can play all the variations of 'Twinkle' without stopping, he shows that he can concentrate four minutes," Suzuki says. His teachers gradually draw the children into longer and longer lessons, and then the parents are able to increase the practice sessions accordingly. I think it is a wondrous thing to see a small child totally absorbed in making music.

Parents' Growing Interest in How Children Learn

Parents have told us that over the years they have become more aware of their children's learning processes and the problems in all of their learning situations, not just the musical ones. They became more and more interested in what and how their children were learning. This increased interest in turn delighted the children and encouraged them to do better.

Exposure to Greatness

The reading of great literature and the study of great art and music have always been considered important influences on people's lives. Suzuki believes that children should have contact with great minds. He says, "Children are taught by Bach, Handel, Vivaldi, Schumann, Mozart and others." When he sees the music of the great composers becoming a part of the children's lives, he is filled with joy, because this love and appreciation will enrich their entire lives.

Long Range Interest in Music

I have been greatly encouraged when I have met some of our young adult graduates who are no longer playing the violin, greatly encouraged because they have expressed a continuing love of music, of Bach, in particular. A young engineer's fond remembrance of the Double Concerto led him to more of Bach's music. A young newspaperwoman attends symphony concerts regularly, and a young mother looks forward to the time when her baby will play the Bach Double Concerto. In these, as in many more young lives, music has continued and will continue to enrich their existence.

Group Lessons, Concerts, Institutes, Social Occasions

Suzuki's group lessons for violinists are really wonderful social affairs bringing together children with a common interest. As in many urban Suzuki programs, our students came from a number of different areas. The group lessons were often the only time these children saw each other. I always liked to give them a little time to socialize before we started. Once we had a visitor who grew a little impatient as I delayed the beginning of the playing. "Just when does this group lesson start?" she asked rather imperiously. "It has already started," I replied, pointing to the clusters of children animatedly catching up on each other's news. "I like this to be an enjoyable experience. I know that the social aspect motivates attendance."

We should be glad that there are other things children enjoy about lessons, concerts and institutes. Most institute directors try to get feedback from the students and parents about the institute experience. In answer to a query about what they liked best about our institute, a great number of the children mentioned our Olympic-size swimming pool! One boy rated the elevator at the top of his list! Still, quite a few especially liked the informal play-ins in the dorm halls at night before bedtime.

Close Parent-Child Relationship

Suzuki lessons do bring parent and child closer together. Although we must admit this increased contact is not always amicable, it does mean that the parent and child will see more of one another. After these years are over so many parents look back on them with nostalgia, forgetting all the struggles that occurred.

One of our mothers whose children are grown and gone comes back occasionally to a concert or play-in. As she watches and listens to the small children play the familiar tunes she recalls what she now remembers as mostly happy days. I met another of our ex-parents recently. I remembered the many painful struggles she'd had with her bright, charming, but willful daughter. I was surprised to see the wistful look on her face as she recalled her daughter's early study!

Now that our youngest is sixteen, we also have our moments of nostalgia. I can't help but tell parents of young children to enjoy all they can as the children progress. In spite of all the troubles, it is a very special time with many possibilities for joy and pleasure.

Parent Absorption—An Island of Repose

Parents who've become absorbed in their children's lessons and those of other children have repeatedly stated that the lessons were often an island of repose for them, drawing their minds from their many cares. I think the secret to this is the fact that they entered into the spirit of the lessons and became absorbed in what was happening. They found themselves rejoicing when a child could finally play a passage correctly after many trials. They felt themselves awed by the capacities of the children and rooted for them intensely.

Entertainment—Lessons, Concerts, At Home

Lessons and concerts in the Suzuki style are very entertaining. The very young children particularly often say and do humorous things.

One little pianist always clapped for herself after performing in a program. At an institute concert, after the solo and violin soloist were announced, the little boy ran up to Connie at the piano and whispered, "How does it go?" One of my very first four-year-old students who seemed to be paying very close attention to everything I was saying and demonstrating, suddenly interrupted me. "I'm going to the foot doctor right after my lesson," she said very seriously.

One evening at a party at our house in Matsumoto, I was demonstrating a prank that I had played on my younger brother. This boy could sleep through every disturbance imaginable. I would stand beside his bed, serenading him on the violin with my special version of the *Star Spangled Banner*, a version in which every second or third note would be out of tune, followed by a few legitimate measures and then more out of tune notes. I was playing this version for the Suzukis when David, our then eighteen-month-old son, came running in from the other room yelling, "Bad! Bad!" He even tried to pull my bow arm down! Suzuki burst into laughter and said, "See! He knows this is bad because he's heard so much good music at home." Suzuki loved to tell this story all over Japan. It showed, he said, the effects of early listening.

We took a group of youngsters to play after dinner on the terrace of our chancellor's house. During the program, I announced 'Andantino' and then proceeded to start the children playing 'Allegretto'. I realized my mistake when I saw the incredulous look on five-year-old Rita's face. She was bursting to tell me that we were playing the wrong piece, but she dutifully kept on playing. When we finished, however, before the guests had a chance to applaud, she burst out, "That was the wrong piece!" Needless to say that took a bit of explaining!

At a demonstration concert we were giving with just two children, Connie and I were to play some of the easier Suzuki tunes after our children had played their portion of the concert. In the middle of

'Humoresque' I went completely blank and came to a sudden halt. I didn't even hear Connie's cueing me at the piano. "Excuse me", I said, "you must remember that I'm not a Suzuki student!" The next try proved successful, but after the program Michael came running up to me. "You didn't forget. How could you forget a piece that you've heard and played so many times?! I think you did that on purpose to show how Suzuki kids remember things much better." I finally persuaded him that I actually *did* forget. "I wonder what you would have thought if we'd have forgotten like that!" he said.

At one of Denda's group concerts in Nagano, Japan, the audience was amused to see a little boy rush up on stage when the next number was announced, start to play with the others, realize almost immediately that he couldn't play that piece, stop and rush back down off the stage, all in the space of about twenty seconds!

Desire to Play

It wasn't until we went to Japan that we were aware of really early participation in concerts. At a violin solo recital in Matsumoto, we watched a tiny three-year-old make her first solo appearance in public. The teacher was right beside her on the stage, making sure of her posture and bow hold. The teacher placed the bow on the string at the tape, then said, "Taka". The little girl played the rhythm of the first variation of Twinkle vigorously, then, placing the violin in rest position, she took a quick bow. Her pigtails bounced in the air. The audience of parents applauded enthusiastically. She looked up in surprise, then hurriedly repositioned her violin and played her encore, a repeat of the Twinkle rhythm!

Most parents who studied an instrument in childhood can remember how they feared playing for people, so the eagerness of Suzuki students in wanting *to play is quite astounding to them. Parents have complained that when they have guests, the children want to perform a whole book of pieces—complained while at the same time were proud! A similar thing occurs after piano play-ins. There is often a scuffle among those who want to play more of their pieces at the piano. Many times during programs the children will ask if they may add another piece to their performance. That's a truly impressive side-effect!*

Projected Adult Activity

The adult who as a child has developed his musical proficiency to a high level will be able to continue it as a hobby or avocation during his adult years if he does not choose it as a career.

Even though I chose music as a profession there have been periods during my life when practice was impossible. Because of what Bill calls "musical money in the bank", my return to playing was not difficult. The years of three and four hours of daily practice during childhood and adolescence, and later extensive practice in music school, built a strong foundation that could be brought out of hibernation.

The amateur musician can do the same if he has developed musical skills to a high level by practicing well through childhood and the teens. In this way music remains a vital part of his life always.

Poise and Self-confidence

Recently some of our Suzuki students participated in an area solo recital in which traditional as well as Suzuki students performed. Before the Suzuki students began to play they bowed quite naturally, adjusted the stool, and paused for mental preparation before they placed their hands on the keyboard. Their generally impressive behavior presented a picture of poise, grace and composure, quite a contrast to the impetuous way many children approach the keyboard.

Ann, a little piano student, demonstrated a wonderful example of composure during a spring recital. She began Mozart's "Arietta", reached the end of the first line and blanked out. Instead of showing signs of panic—the fumbling and chaotic searching that is often the hallmark of a situation like this—she quietly returned her hands to her lap and repeated her preparation again. She began once more only to reach the same impasse. I was sitting close to her, so I whispered, "Would you like me to help you?" "Yes", she whispered in return. I went up behind her, and played pianissimo past the part she had missed.

*She smiled, started again and played a fine performance from begin-
ning to end. This was an excellent example of the kind of poise and
self-confidence that is evident within the child who is a Suzuki student.
Afterward I thanked her for her wonderful recovery and told her how
proud I was of her performance.*

Respect of Peers

Peer attention during school years comes mainly from participation in sports. The fact that music performers can gain the respect
and admiration of their contemporaries may seem unlikely to those
who haven't seen it, but it is possible.

Our Judith, 10, was asked to perform a violin solo on a school
assembly program. She was in the fifth grade and a bit skeptical
about her reception from her peers. Bach's A Minor Concerto was her
choice because she knew it well, not because it was a hit parade
selection! Her performance was filled with vitality. There was such
excitement in her playing that the kids in the audience were caught
up in it. When she finished, they clapped with so much enthusiasm
and for such a long time that the adults were all amazed. This
demonstrated that even young children recognize exciting accomplishment in their peers.

Many Suzuki students have been surprised at the attention they
have gotten from students and teachers when they have played at
their schools. One mother reported that after her child played for her
class, she received so many compliments that she said to her mother
incredulously, "Gosh, I didn't know I was *that* good!"

Memory Development

Memory is the necessary ingredient of all learning, although not
long ago educators de-emphasized its importance, giving higher
priority to the development of creative thought. Why should they be
mutually exclusive? I think creative thought must have stored material to give it substance. We must have input before we can have
output!

The Talent Education kindergarten's emphasis on, for one thing, memorization of the Japanese poem, the haiku, gives the very young child the memory exercise that helps generate his later success in school, in all subjects at all levels.

The growth of memory capabilities is also present in Suzuki music study. Again and again stories are told with incredulity about children who memorize orchestra parts after several playings, or who learn a book or two of music in fantastically short periods of time.

On an afternoon recital, a student string quartet was to perform a movement of a Haydn quartet. The second violinist, as she walked into the room, gave a horrified gasp. "I've forgotten my music!" There was no time to return home for it, and no other copy was available. "Do you think you could remember your part?" the cellist asked. "I'll try." It was quite a demonstration, especially for the adult musicians present. The quartet performed with no problem. The little 'absent-minded' musician was not 'absent-minded' at all. She was very 'present-minded' as she played her part from memory!

The memory develops and grows with use. Suzuki training provides fertile ground for its flowering.

Playing Together

Making music together is one of the greatest joys for the amateur as well as the professional musician. The Suzuki string player has wonderful experiences in playing with others in group lessons. Later he can participate in orchestras and in chamber groups. Even his solos are ensemble experiences because an accompanist is usually required.

The pianist is not so fortunate. As soon as he can read music well, however, he can play duets and accompany on an elementary level. Later, he too will be able to participate in chamber groups, usually with string players.

Musicians feel that ensemble playing makes the musician. One cannot go one's own merry way, (as pianists often do) but must listen to all the other parts as they relate to the whole. Aside from the enjoyment involved, ensemble playing develops sensitivity and maturity in the musician.

A Chance to Give

Many Suzuki students have had the opportunity to experience the joy of giving happiness to people outside of their own families. Students have many opportunities to perform as soloists and in groups but one of the most gratifying is playing for senior citizens in nursing and retirement homes. In Knoxville, our Suzuki students played at regular intervals during the year for a nursing home. The staff said that the turnout for these programs was larger and more enthusiastic than for any other program presented there. The appreciative smiling faces, the sincere compliments, the loving gestures of the audience gave the children a joyful experience—that of being able to give something unique and special to someone.

Benefits for Parents

When we enroll one or more of our children in Suzuki study, we are putting ourselves and our children into a position wherein all may accrue many benefits, quite a number of them not directly related to developing the ability to play well. We will learn much about music, about our children, how skills are acquired, the tremendous effect of the environment on the learning process, and the importance of a healthy self-image in ourselves as well as our children.

Watching the changing attitudes of parents and teachers toward children, I wonder if Suzuki might not have had an ulterior motive aside from "the happiness of all children". Perhaps it could have been "for the character formation of all parents and teachers."

Suzuki has generated for the world the birth of belief in the potential greatness of each small child and the joy of nurturing that seed of greatness. The growth of love and the gratitude and respect for the gifts that God has bestowed on all of us make life the exciting adventure it should be. It is this celebration of life that is the magnet that draws people of all nations and creeds to Suzuki and his Talent Education. It is for this that we, parents and teachers, now and in the future, shall be eternally grateful to him.

238

GENERAL BIBLIOGRAPHY

Ball, Vernon. *Alpha Backgammon.* New York: William Morrow, 1980.

Billings, Helen K. *A Priceless Educational Advantage.* Ft. Lauderdale, Florida: Helen K. Billings Foundation, 1976.

Briggs, Dorothy Corkille. *Your Child's Self-Esteem.* New York: Doubleday, 1975.

Brown, Barbara. *New Mind, New Body.* New York: Harper and Row, 1974.

Buscaglia, Leo. *Living, Loving, and Learning.* New York: Ballentine Books, 1982.

Carton, Lonnie. *Raise Your Kids Right.* New York: Putnam, 1980.

Campbell, Ross. *How to Really Love Your Child.* Wheaton, Ill: Victor Books, 1977.

Campbell, Ross. *How to Really Love Your Teenager.* Wheaton, Ill: Victor Books, 1981.

Cook, Clifford A. *Suzuki Education in Action.* New York: Exposition Press, 1970.

Cratty, Bryant J. *Psychology and Physical Activity.* Englewood Cliffs, N.J.: Prentice-Hall, 1968.

Cratty, Bryant J. *Psychomotor Behavior in Education and Sport.* Springfield, Ill.: Charles Thomas, 1974.

Dechant, Emerald V. *Improving the Teaching of Reading.* Englewood Cliffs, N.J.: Prentice-Hall, 1964.

Dobson, James. *Hide or Seek.* Old Tappan, N.J.: Fleming H. Revell, 1974.

Dobson, James. *The Strong-Willed Child.* Wheaton, Ill.: Tyndale House, 1978.

Dolch, E. W. *Psychology and Teaching of Reading.* Champaign, Ill.: The Garrard Press, 1951.

Gallwey, W. Timothy. *Inner Tennis.* New York: Random House, 1976.

Ginott, Haim. *Between Parent and Child.* New York: MacMillan, 1965.

Gordon, Arthur. *A Touch of Wonder.* Old Tappan, N.J.: Fleming H. Revell, 1974.

Green, Elmer and Alyce. *Beyond Biofeedback.* New York: Dell Publishing Co., 1977.

Hart, Hornell. *Autoconditioning.* Englewood Cliffs, N.J.: Prentice-Hall, 1956.

Holding, Dennis H. *Human Skills.* New York: J. Wiley, 1981.

Kataoka, Eiko and Masayoshi, editors. *Talent Education Journal.* St. Louis, 1979.

Kohl, Herbert R. *Reading, How to.* New York: Dutton, 1973.

Kuzma, Kay. *Working Mothers.* New York: Rawson, Wade Publishers, 1980.

Lawther, John Dobson. *Learning of Physical Skills.* Englewood Cliffs, N.J.: Prentice-Hall, 1968.

Lawther, John Dobson. *Sports Psychology.* Englewood Cliffs, N.J.: Prentice-Hall, 1972.

Maltz, Maxwell. *The Magic Power of Self-Image Psychology.* Englewood Cliffs, N.J.: Prentice-Hall, 1964.

Mednick, Sarnoff A. *Learning.* Englewood Cliffs, N.J.: Prentice-Hall, 1964.

Montessori, Maria. *What You Should Know About Your Child.* India: Kalakshetra Publications, 1961.

Mursell, J. L. *Music Education: Principles and Programs.* New York: Silver Burdette, 1956.

Oxendine, Joseph. *Psychology of Motor Learning.* New York: Appleton-Century Crofts, 1968.

Petzold, Robert G. *The Perception of Music Symbols in Music Reading by Normal Children and Children Gifted Musically.* Journal of Experimental Education 28:272, June, 1960.

Robb, Margaret. *The Dynamics of Motor-Skill Acquisition.* Englewood Cliffs, N.J.: Prentice-Hall, 1972.

Rosenthal, Robert, and Jacobson, Lenore. *Pygmalion in the Classroom.* New York: Holt, Rinehart, and Winston, 1968.

Schultz, Johannes, and Luthe, Wolfgang. *Autogenic Training: Psychophysiologic Approach in Psychotherapy.* New York: Grune and Stratton, 1959.

Singer, Robert N. *The Psychomotor Domain.* Washington: Gryphon House, 1972.

Starr, William J. *The Suzuki Violinist.* Knoxville, TN: Kingston Ellis Press, 1976.

Suinn, Richard J., editor. *Psychology in Sports.* Minneapolis: Burgess, 1980.

Suzuki, Shinichi. *Nurtured by Love.* New York: Exposition Press, 1969.

Tinker, Miles. *Bases for Effective Reading.* Minneapolis: U. of Minnesota Press, 1965.

Tohei, Koichi. *Book of Ki.* Tokyo: Japan Publications, 1976.

Wiener, Norbert. *Cybernetics.* Cambridge: M.I.T. Press, 1965.

Westrup, J.A., and Harrison, F.L. *Notation.* The New College Encyclopedia of Music. New York: W.W. Norton, 1960.

NUTRITIONAL BIBLIOGRAPHY

Abrahmson, E.M., M.D., and Pezet, A.W. *Body, Mind & Sugar.* New York: Avon Books, 1951.

Davis, Adelle. *Let's Eat Right to Keep Fit.* New York: Harcourt Brace Jovanovich, Inc., 1954.

Dufty, William. *Sugar Blues.* Radnor, Pa.: Chilton Book Co., 1975.

Feingold, Ben F., and Helene S. *The Feingold Cookbook for Hyperactive Children.* New York: Random House, 1979.

Kinderlehrer, Jane. *Confessions of a Sneaky Organic Cook.* Emmaus, Pa.: Rodale Press, Inc., 1971.

Pickard, Mary Ann. *Feasting Naturally.* Lenexa, Kansas: Cookbook Publishers, Inc., 1979.

Pickard, Mary Ann. *Feasting Naturally From Your Own Recipes.* Lenexa, Kansas: Cookbook Publishers, Inc., 1981.

Pickard, Mary Ann. *Feasting Naturally With Our Friends.* Lenexa, Kansas: Cookbook Publishers, Inc., 1982.

Sloan, Sara. *A Guide for Nutra Lunches and Natural Foods.* Atlanta: SOS Printing, 1977.

Smith, Lendon H., M.D. *Improving Your Child's Behavior Chemistry.* Englewood Cliffs, N.J.: Prentice-Hall, 1976.

Smith, Lendon H., M.D. *Feed Your Kinds Right.* New York: Dell, 1979.

APPENDIX

Publications in the Suzuki field by Kingston Ellis Press.

Audiocasette tapes:

SUZUKI SPEAKS TO PARENTS

This is a conversation between Shinichi Suzuki and William Starr made in Suzuki's studio in Matsumoto in 1969.

GIVE YOUR CHILD A PRICELESS EDUCATIONAL ADVANTAGE AT HOME, FREE
This tape, made by Dr. Billings herself, is a digest of her book of the same title.

Books:

THE SUZUKI VIOLINIST by William Starr
Already a classic, this guide for teachers and parents is used in the Americas, Europe, and Australia. Teachers have found this book an invaluable aid and continue to recommend it enthusiastically to parents of their students.

THE MUSIC ROAD, BOOKS 1 AND 2 by Constance Starr
An antidote to "Why Johnny Can't Read - Music". These volumes provide the same repetition and review to develop music reading skills that the Suzuki student has already employed in learning to perform the Suzuki repertoire.

TWENTY-SIX COMPOSERS TEACH THE VIOLINIST
by William Starr
A book of excerpts from solo, chamber and orchestral literature supplementing the Suzuki books at the Book VI level. Carefully compiled and edited, the material covers a great range of technical problems.